GAZALA 1942

Rommel's greatest victory

CAMPAIGN • 196

GAZALA 1942

Rommel's greatest victory

KEN FORD

ILLUSTRATED BY JOHN WHITE

Series editors Marcus Cowper and Nikolai Bogdanovic

First published in Great Britain in 2008 by Osprey Publishing
Midland House, West Way, Botley, Oxford OX2 0PH, UK
443 Park Avenue South, New York, NY 10016, USA
E-mail: info@ospreypublishing.com

A CIP catalogue record for this book is available from the British Library.

ISBN 978 1 84603 264 6

Editorial by Ilios Publishing Ltd, Oxford, UK (www.iliospublishing.com)
Page layout by The Black Spot
Index by Alison Worthington
Typeset in Sabon and Mriad Pro
Maps by The Map Studio Ltd
3D bird's-eye views by The Black Spot
Battlescene illustrations by John White
Originated by United Graphic Pte Ltd.
Printed in China through Worldprint

08 09 10 11 12   10 9 8 7 6 5 4 3 2 1

FOR A CATALOGUE OF ALL BOOKS PUBLISHED BY OSPREY MILITARY AND
AVIATION PLEASE CONTACT:

NORTH AMERICA
Osprey Direct, c/o Random House Distribution Center, 400 Hahn Road,
Westminster, MD 21157
E-mail: Info@ospreydirect.com

ALL OTHER REGIONS
Osprey Direct UK, P.O. Box 140 Wellingborough, Northants, NN8 2FA, UK
E-mail: info@ospreydirect.co.uk

www.ospreypublishing.com

ACKNOWLEDGEMENTS

I should like to express my gratitude to the Trustees of the Imperial War
Museum, the Commonwealth War Graves Commission and to Steve Bulpit
for permission to use the photographs for which they hold the copyright.

ARTIST'S NOTE

Readers may care to note that the original paintings from which the
colour plates in this book were prepared are available for private sale.
All reproduction copyright whatsoever is retained by the Publishers.
All enquiries should be addressed to:

John White
5107 C Monroe Road
Charlotte
NC 28205
USA

The Publishers regret that they can enter into no correspondence upon
this matter.

THE WOODLAND TRUST

Osprey Publishing are supporting the Woodland Trust, the UK's leading
woodland conservation charity, by funding the dedication of trees.

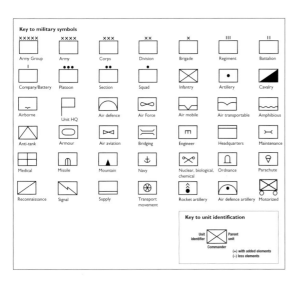

CONTENTS

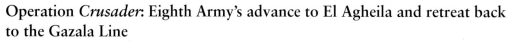

Operation *Crusader*: Eighth Army's advance to El Agheila and retreat back to the Gazala Line

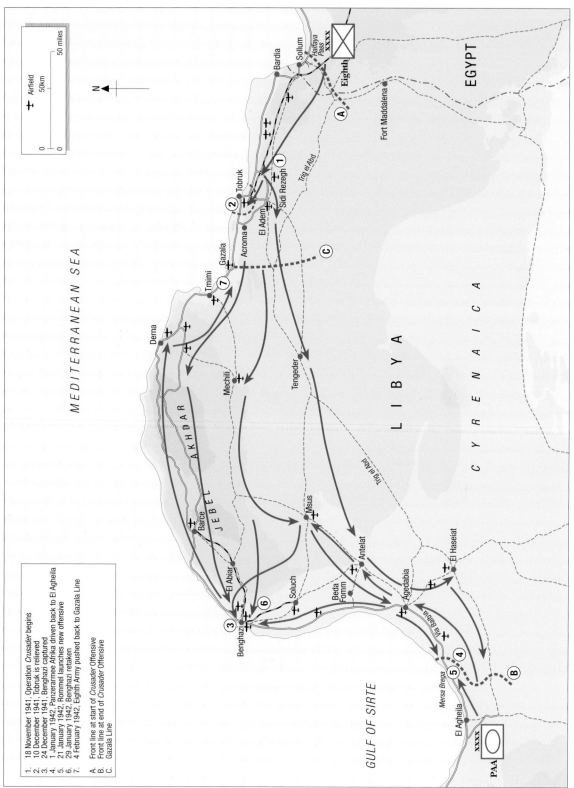

Scale/Legend:
- ✈ Airfield
- 50km
- 50 miles

N ←

Key:
1. 18 November 1941, Operation *Crusader* begins
2. 10 December 1941, Tobruk is relieved
3. 24 December 1941, Benghazi captured
4. 1 January 1942, Panzerarmee Afrika driven back to El Agheila
5. 21 January 1942, Rommel launches new offensive
6. 29 January 1942, Benghazi retaken
7. 4 February 1942, Eighth Army pushed back to Gazala Line

A. Front line at start of *Crusader* Offensive
B. Front line at end of *Crusader* Offensive
C. Gazala Line

Map labels:
MEDITERRANEAN SEA
EGYPT
LIBYA
CYRENAICA
GULF OF SIRTE
JEBEL AKHDAR
Trig el Abd

Bardia, Sollum, Halfaya Pass, Fort Maddalena, Tobruk, Sidi Rezegh, El Adem, Acroma, Gazala, Tmimi, Derna, Mechili, Tengeder, El Haseiat, Antelat, Agedabia, Via Balbia, Beda Fomm, Soluch, Benghazi, El Abiar, Barce, Msus, Mersa Brega, El Agheila

Eighth — XXXX
PAA — XXXX

ORIGINS OF THE BATTLE

Generalfeldmarschall Rommel strikes a defiant pose for the camera on the main coastal road across Libya to Egypt, the Via Balbia, which formed the main axis for the to-and-fro battles that took place in North Africa between 1940 and 1943. (IWM, HU5623)

The start of 1942 marked the third calendar year of the war in the North African desert. What had begun as border skirmishes between two colonial powers on 11 June 1940, the day after Italy had declared war on Britain, later developed into a full-scale theatre of war which pitted British and Commonwealth forces against the fascist empire of the Axis regimes.

It had all started so well for General Archibald Wavell's sparse Western Desert Force. His two divisions pushed the seven divisions of Graziani's Italian Tenth Army back across Libya to El Agheila at the base of the Gulf of Sirte, capturing great numbers of troops and equipment in the process. Wavell's force was then plagued by the same problems that were to affect both sides throughout the desert war; how to supply their armies on the front line when their supply trains stretched back hundreds of kilometres in the rear? Everything from ammunition to toilet paper had to be ferried forwards across featureless terrain, along poor roads and through shifting desert. The farther west the British advanced, the longer the supply train grew, sucking in more and more men and transport just to keep those at the front sustained.

Wavell paused at El Agheila and tried to build his strength prior to resuming his westward advance. By this time his force had become XIII Corps under the command of Lieutenant-General Richard O'Connor and comprised 6th Australian Division and 7th Armoured Division. At this point Axis forces invaded Greece and Prime Minister Churchill instructed Wavell to send part of his strength to help counter enemy forces there. Lieutenant-General O'Connor was ordered to relinquish the Australian Division and part of 7th Armoured Division, which left him with few forces to hold the line. Worse was to follow when Hitler came to the aid of his Italian ally and dispatched Generalleutnant Erwin Rommel to North Africa in a bid to restore some prestige to the Axis cause. With Rommel came the fledgling units that were to form the Afrika Korps – just part of the 5.leichte Division and elements of 15.Panzer Division – but they were enough to bolster the Italians into launching an attack against the British on 24 March 1941.

With Rommel's armoured cars leading the assault, Axis forces pushed the British XIII Corps right back to the Egyptian border and, by 14 April, had cleared the whole of Cyrenaica save for a beleaguered garrison of two Australian brigades holed up in the port of Tobruk. The rapid advance now left Rommel with long supply lines to the rear and little extra strength, fuel or ammunition to push farther eastwards into Egypt. His advance halted at the Halfaya Pass. In contrast, Wavell's forces had short lines of

communication and were growing stronger by the day as new formations arrived in Egypt from Britain and the Commonwealth.

Wavell struck back on 15 May with Operation *Brevity* in which he tried to repossess the strategically important Halfaya Pass. Initially, the attack was successful, but within 12 days Rommel counterattacked and took it back again. Wavell tried again on 15 June with a more ambitious strike named Operation *Battleaxe*. The results were the same: Rommel's defensive tactics had the measure of the attack and the battle was virtually over in just two days with the vital pass remaining in Axis hands. Rommel had the strength to resist the British, but had little extra might with which to force his way into Egypt. Reinforcement seemed unlikely, for seven days later Hitler launched his attack on Russia and the Afrika Korps slipped down the list of German priorities.

Churchill now lost patience with Wavell and replaced him with General Sir Claude Auchinleck. During that summer the Western Desert Force was enlarged by the addition of XXX Corps and became Eighth Army with Lieutenant-General Alan Cunningham, recent victor against the Italians in Abyssinia, in command. A new, much larger offensive, Operation *Crusader*, was planned to begin on 18 November. This time Auchinleck and Cunningham would begin by trying to outflank Rommel's positions at the Halfaya Pass and drive through to Tobruk. At the same time, the Tobruk garrison would break out of its encirclement to join up with Eighth Army. While this offensive was being planned, Rommel himself was organizing his own attack aimed against Tobruk, convinced that the British posed no serious threat to him.

Cunningham struck first and succeeded in launching XXX Corps behind the enemy at Halfaya Pass and swung out into the desert. Rommel met this attack at Sidi Rezegh and caused great damage to the inferior British armour, destroying the bulk of XXX Corps' tanks. The German commander now had an opportunity to annihilate XXX Corps, but chose to attempt a greater victory by attacking eastwards in an effort to get behind the rear of Eighth Army and cut its line of retreat in order to destroy it completely.

The move unnerved Cunningham who then urged Auchinleck to sanction a general retreat. Auchinleck was made of sterner stuff and refused to give way, reasoning that Rommel's forces must now be tired and in as bad a way

Italian troops man a Breda 20/65 model 35 cannon. This 20mm gun was designed in 1934 as an anti-aircraft weapon, but had a dual role in the desert where it served as an anti-tank gun, albeit with a poor reputation and inferior performance when compared with most other weapons. (IWM, MH5867)

as the British. He ordered every unit to attack the enemy and to pursue him relentlessly and then replaced Cunningham with his own Deputy Chief of Staff, Lieutenant-General Neil Ritchie. Rommel's attempt to disorganize the British partially succeeded, but it also caused some confusion within his own army. He failed to achieve his plans on two counts: he was not strong enough to break the British positions, nor did he have sufficient forces opposite Tobruk to hold the British down in his rear.

Although Ritchie was titular head of Eighth Army, it was Auchinleck who now directed the course of the battle with orders for a resumption of the attack on Sidi Rezegh. The move unbalanced the Axis command for Rommel was still well to the east and out of touch with his main headquarters. Days of intense and confused fighting followed as Rommel tried to take back the initiative. Great damage was suffered by both sides fighting furiously to gain control of the battlefield. Ritchie's troops pushed on to Tobruk and managed to lift the siege. Gradually the superior strength of the British began to overcome Rommel's command and the Afrika Korps was in danger of being surrounded. Rommel tried one last attack to break through into Tobruk on 5 December but it failed. The next day he ordered a general retreat.

The British chased Rommel back across Cyrenaica, past Benghazi right back to El Agheila where his advance had started the previous March. Each time the pursuing Eighth Army got too close, the Afrika Korps would turn round and deliver a sharp rebuff. By the start of January 1942 most of Rommel's forces were ensconced in the old Axis positions along the El Agheila–Marada strongpoint facing eastwards ready to fight a defensive battle against Lt. Gen. Ritchie's army. Here, with much shorter supply lines to their bases in Tripolitania, Axis forces quickly began to replenish their losses and rebuild their strength.

Although Operation *Crusader* was costly to Eighth Army in men and equipment, its effort was rewarded with a decisive victory over the seemingly invincible Rommel and his Afrika Korps. Both sides were equal in strength at the start of the battle on 18 November, with the British and Commonwealth forces numbering 118,000 men and the Axis forces 119,000. When the fighting was over, British losses amounted to 17,700 and the enemy losses 24,500, of which 14,600 were German. Rommel was not, however, defeated. His command was intact and, although his force was exhausted, it still had plenty of fight left in it. The victory had been a great boost for Eighth Army's morale, for Ritchie's troops had thrown the enemy out of Cyrenaica and relieved Tobruk. His officers and their men now felt that they had the capability of beating Rommel and evicting Axis forces from North Africa. In this they were quite wrong, for Rommel had no intention of letting Eighth Army rest on its laurels and build up strength for another offensive.

On 5 January 1942 a convoy arrived in North Africa, which landed 54 German tanks and 20 armoured cars as well as a sizeable number of anti-aircraft and artillery guns. Also being shipped in to Rommel were large quantities of fuel and ammunition. With these reinforcements he began thinking of going back on the offensive. Intelligence led the German commander to believe that the British outposts were thinly held and widely dispersed. By the middle of January Rommel decided he was strong enough to mount an attack.

Auchinleck was oblivious to this quick turnaround in Axis fortunes, for both he and his commanders believed that it would be almost impossible for Rommel to take the offensive for some considerable time. Their intelligence had shown them that his losses, his lack of reinforcements and his supply difficulties would make further aggressive moves difficult for him. When Rommel struck early on the morning of 21 January, just 16 days after the last of his rearguard had retired behind the El Agheila defences, British Eighth Army was taken completely by surprise.

There had been some changes made to Eighth Army formations since the end of the *Crusader* battle, with the veteran 7th Armoured Division being

A gun from the 'Bush Artillery' in action during the long siege of Tobruk. The 'unit' was made up of engineers and infantry who used captured Italian field guns to supplement the work of the regular artillery during the nine months that Tobruk was cut off from Eighth Army. The gunners here are firing a captured Italian 75mm gun to good effect. (IWM, E4788)

withdrawn to be replaced by the untried and understrength 1st Armoured Division. Its 2nd Armoured Brigade had no desert experience and had had little training since arriving in Egypt the previous month, but was sent forwards to hold the front line. Fuel shortages meant that Ritchie could also maintain just one infantry brigade in a forward position, so that when Rommel launched his attack there was little to stop him making quick gains.

A speedy withdrawal saved the British advance forces from complete destruction, but allowed Rommel to motor northwards at speed. In eight days Axis forces had retaken Benghazi and Rommel had swung his troops eastwards, pushing Ritchie's army back towards Tobruk. Lack of fuel slowed down the strength of the Axis advance, which in turn allowed the British XIII Corps to withdraw into the safety of the partially prepared Gazala–Bir Hacheim defence line, just 64km to the west of Tobruk. Rommel had engineered an impressive advance and a great tactical victory. In just over two weeks, and with almost negligible losses, the Axis commander had driven Eighth Army back over 560km and had retaken much of the ground lost during the British *Crusader* offensive.

There now followed a period during which both sides rested, trained their forces and prepared to launch a new offensive. Rommel and Auchinleck both knew that the other would attack when he was ready and each hoped that he would be the one who was ready first. On 26 May, Rommel won the race and attacked.

A Matilda infantry tank of the type used by the British Army tank brigades during the Gazala battle. The Matilda was the heaviest and best-protected tank on the battlefield having 78mm armour at its thickest point, a level of protection not matched by any of the Axis tanks. Its main weapon, however, was the 2-pdr gun that proved to be woefully inadequate when facing German armour. (IWM, E9560)

CHRONOLOGY

1941

18 November   Under command of Lt. Gen. Alan Cunningham, British Eighth Army launches Operation *Crusader* against Axis forces led by Gen. Erwin Rommel to join up with the besieged garrison in Tobruk

26 November   After protracted and confused fighting during which time the British fail to press the offensive hard enough to achieve a result, the C-in-C Middle East, Gen. Claude Auchinleck, decides to replace Cunningham at the head of Eighth Army with Lt. Gen. Neil Ritchie.

10 December   Further prolonged fighting results in Rommel beginning to withdraw eastwards and Tobruk is relieved after a siege that had lasted eight months.

1942

1 January   Rommel's forces are chased back across Cyrenaica into his old positions at El Agheila where he had started his advance ten months before.

21 January   To the surprise of many within Eighth Army, Rommel resumes the offensive and pushes back the British, forcing them to withdraw across the very ground they had recently won.

4 February   The retreat becomes a flight and Eighth Army are compelled to withdraw into prepared positions at Gazala, 64km to the east of Tobruk

February–May   A period of rest and replenishment is taken by both sides as they prepare to go on the offensive once again.

26 May   Rommel strikes first and launches an attack against the northern section of Eighth Army's line with his mainly Italian Gruppe Crüwell.

27 May   Early in the morning Rommel leads a mobile armoured force around the southern flank of the British line. Ritchie tries to counter this move with his armoured brigades.

28 May   Rommel's planned move to get behind the bulk of Eighth Army starts to fail as British tanks and guns slow his forward movement. Rommel regroups his forces ready for another attack.

29 May   Rommel decides to bring his armour into an area later to be called the Cauldron, a position that is virtually surrounded by Eighth Army, but one from which he can strike eastwards when the time is right. As he withdraws into this position his rear comes into contact with a defended 'box' manned by Brigadier Haydon's 150th Brigade.

30 May	Rommel attempts to eliminate 150th Brigade's position and open up supply routes to the west through the British minefields. Ritchie now thinks he has Rommel trapped and launches new attacks to crush the Afrika Korps, but they lack strength and are easily repulsed.
31 May	While Rommel continues to batter away at the 150th Brigade 'box', Ritchie plans another attack on the Cauldron.
1 June	Brigadier Haydon is killed and the survivors of 150th Brigade surrender, Ritchie still does not attack the Cauldron in force. Rommel now has a direct supply route eastwards through the minefields and is no longer surrounded.
3 June	Rommel holds the British armour in the centre and dispatches forces southwards to overrun the Free French outpost at Bir Hacheim.
5 June	Ritchie launches Operation *Aberdeen* to crush Rommel's position in the Cauldron. Rommel holds the attack and then launches a counterattack against the British armour, chasing away three armoured brigades and capturing large numbers of infantry.
10 June	The Bir Hacheim position of the Free French is overrun and captured.
11 June	Rommel once more concentrates his mobile forces and moves against the centre of the British rear. He is met by Norrie's XXX Corps and stopped, but again with great loss to the British tank force.
12 June	A great clash of armour to the south of Knightsbridge is decisive; British losses force a withdrawal to the north and east, leaving those formations of Eighth Army to the west vulnerable.

13 June	The 201st Guards Brigade is forced to retreat from the Knightsbridge defensive position in the centre of the British line.
14 June	Rommel's forces begin to pick off the isolated positions west of Tobruk and the 50th and 1st South African divisions begin to withdraw from the Gazala Line. Eighth Army is in danger of collapse.
17 June	Rommel's forces make it to the sea to the east of Tobruk and once more the port is surrounded. All those units of Eighth Army that are able retreat back to the Egyptian border.
20 June	Tobruk is attacked from the east by the Afrika Korps. A break-in is soon achieved and Axis forces quickly spread out within the fortress area.
21 June	Major-General Klopper surrenders the Tobruk garrison.
22 June	German troops cross the frontier into Egypt. Eighth Army continues its withdrawal into the defences south of Mersa Matruh.
26 June	Rommel begins his attack on the British positions at Matruh.
28 June	The Matruh position is given up and Auchinleck orders all units to retire eastwards behind the El Alamein Line.
30 June	All units of Eighth Army that have survived the long retreat are now behind the El Alamein Line waiting for Rommel to launch his next attack.

OPPOSING COMMANDERS

The battle of Gazala was Rommel's greatest triumph in North Africa. His handling of the campaign and the relentless pressure that he applied to British Eighth Army marked him out as a great armoured commander. In contrast, despite the overwhelming force available to Lt. Gen. Ritchie, he was never able to grasp the initiative fully and apply the knock-out blow to Panzerarmee Afrika. The battle was fought as Rommel dictated with the British generals having to react to the German commander's moves.

BRITISH COMMANDERS

General Sir Claude Auchinleck, British C-in-C Middle East Command. His task of halting Rommel's progress towards Egypt with inferior equipment, his lack of skilful subordinate commanders and his attempts to stave off Churchill's never-ending calls for precipitate action, made his command an onerous and demanding one. (IWM, E13794)

Compared with the brilliant exponent of armour warfare at the head of Axis forces, British Eighth Army had few armoured leaders of note. Neither Gen. Auchinleck nor Lt. Gen. Ritchie was fully conversant with the deployment of tank formations, nor had they learned from the armoured disasters of their predecessors in the desert.

General Sir Claude Auchinleck (1884–1981) had been made Commander-in-Chief Middle East to replace Gen. Sir Archibald Wavell, who was dismissed after his failed attempts to raise the Axis siege of the port of Tobruk in July 1941. He had spent most of his army life in the Indian Army and began World War II on the subcontinent as Commander Meerut District. Auchinleck was moved to the Middle East from his position as C-in-C India. He had held this command after his leadership of the abortive Anglo-French campaign in Norway in 1940. As C-in-C Middle East his responsibilities included not only the battleground of North Africa, but also the trouble spots of Palestine, Iraq and Persia. He was a modest, rather austere individual who shunned publicity. An able and well-respected commander, he lacked Rommel's forceful personality and grasp of armoured tactics.

Lieutenant-General Neil Ritchie (1897–1985) was given command of Eighth Army at a time of crisis during the *Crusader* offensive. Up until that time he had only commanded at battalion level in the field and his elevation to army command was originally seen as just a temporary one. After the success of the *Crusader* operation Auchinleck decided to make Ritchie's command permanent, fearing that yet another change at the head of Eighth Army might affect morale.

Ritchie had been commissioned into the Black Watch in December 1914. During World War I he served on the Western Front and was wounded in the battle of Loos in 1915. Later in the war he served in Mesopotamia and took part in Allenby's campaign in Palestine during which time he was awarded the

Distinguished Service Order and the Military Cross. Early in World War II he served on Alanbrooke's staff in France in 1940 and, post-Dunkirk, helped to re-form the 51st Highland Division after the original formation had surrendered to Rommel at St Valéry. He later joined Wavell at Middle East Command as Deputy Chief of General Staff, just before the arrival of Auchinleck. He therefore lacked experience of handling large formations in battle and, as an infantryman, had virtually no knowledge regarding the tactical employment of armoured units.

Fortunately, both of Ritchie's corps commanders had tank experience. **Lieutenant-General Charles Willoughby Norrie (1893–1977)** was a cavalryman who had served in tanks during World War I. He spent the middle part of his career as a commander of cavalry at battalion and brigade level. When war broke out he held brigade command in the 2nd Armoured Division in England. In August 1940 he took over the 1st Armoured Division, moving with the formation to Egypt in late 1941. On arrival in the Middle East in November 1941 he was immediately elevated to corps command at the head of XXX Corps to replace the recently killed Lieutenant-General Vyvyan Pope.

Lieutenant-General William 'Strafer' Gott (1897–1942) had been in the desert since the outbreak of war. He began 1939 at the head of a motor infantry battalion of the Armoured Division (Egypt), which was later enlarged to become 7th Armoured Division. He then successively commanded, 7th Support Group, 7th Armoured Division and XIII Corps, and fought in all the major engagements of the Desert War. By the time of the Gazala battles Gott had become Eighth Army's most experienced tank commander, but was by then strained from the non-stop ebb and flow of action with the Italians and Germans.

Of the armoured division commanders, **Major-General Frank Messervy (1893–1974)** was another infantryman who had recently been commander of the 4th Indian Division during the fighting in Ethiopia before assuming command of 7th Armoured Division. Up until then he had not led armoured formations in action. **Major-General Herbert Lumsden (1897–1945)** was a cavalryman who had commanded an armoured brigade in England before taking over 1st Armoured Division in Egypt at the end of 1941. Gazala was, for both of these commanders, their first experience of armoured warfare.

Ritchie's divisional commanders contained just one man with any experience of fighting Rommel, **Major-General Dan Pienaar (1893–1942)**. The 1st South African Division's commander was a prickly and somewhat forceful individual, but he did at least have some knowledge of the desert. Pienaar had previously commanded an infantry brigade in the Eritrea and Ethiopia campaigns and had then taken part in the *Crusader* offensive. Pienaar was not generally well liked by his fellow commanders and his relationship with Gott was very strained. Commanding 2nd South African Division in Tobruk was **Major-General H. Klopper (1902–1978)** who had been in North Africa only a short time. The 50th Division had **Major-General William Ramsden** at its head who had arrived in Libya in February 1942 after a roundabout trip from the UK via Cyprus, Iraq and Syria. Ramsden had seen some action leading an infantry brigade in France in 1940.

Commanding the 1ère Brigade Française Libre, who garrisoned the defensive position at Bir Hacheim on the extreme southern end of the Gazala Line, was **Général de brigade Marie Pierre Koenig (1898–1970)**. He had served with distinction as a junior officer in World War I. In 1940 he was part of the French contingent during the Norwegian campaign and took part

Lieutenant-General Neil Ritchie, Commander British Eighth Army. Ritchie was summoned from a staff appointment in Cairo to take command of Britain's most important army in the field against one of the world's best armoured leaders, even though he had never before commanded anything larger than a battalion in action and had no experience of tank warfare. (IWM, E9568)

Lieutenant-General Norrie, Commander XXX Corps. (IWM, E13290)

in countering the German invasion of France, escaping to England via Dunkirk to join Général Charles de Gaulle's Free French forces in London. He later served in Syria and Lebanon with the Free French 1ère Division.

If the generals at the top were short of experience in command of armoured formations, many of the junior commanders at brigade and battalion level made up for that shortcoming. Men like Brigadier Raymond Briggs of 2nd Armoured Brigade and Lieutenant-Colonel G. P. B. 'Pip' Roberts of the 3rd Royal Tank Regiment. Roberts in particular was impressive in action and rose to command 11th Armoured Division in North-west Europe, ending the war as one of Britain's best divisional generals.

AXIS COMMANDERS

Although Panzerarmee Afrika was a formation of both Italian and German forces with the bulk of its troops being Italian, its command was German, its strategy was German inspired and its tactical deployment was German led. At its head was one of the best German armoured commanders of the war.

Generaloberst Erwin Rommel (1891–1944) began 1942 as Commander Panzergruppe Afrika, but this formation was elevated to army status after it had driven the British from Tripolitania to become Panzerarmee Afrika in February 1942. Rommel's reputation had grown significantly since arriving in North Africa the previous year. His masterly use of mobile forces against the British had earned him almost legendary status with those on both sides of the conflict.

Rommel was already held in high regard by many within the Nazi hierarchy as well among his contemporaries in the Wehrmacht. During World War I as a battalion commander he won Germany's highest award for bravery, the Pour le Mérite, and later produced a book of his experiences, *Infanterie greift an* (*Infantry Tactics*), which helped to single him out as a very special commander of men. His later service at the head of Hitler's security battalion gave him the further advantage of being well regarded by the Führer himself.

Rommel came to the North African theatre with a good deal of experience of handling armoured formations in France. He was a master of bold manoeuvre and incisive attack, believing that audacity and resolve on the battlefield invariably unbalanced the opposition. He was quick to learn that the British commanders who faced him across the desert were not of the same calibre; they were men who rarely took risks, preferring to wait until they had amassed overwhelming strength with which to grind down the opposition.

Rommel was very much in command of the actual fighting in the desert, but the strategy of the campaign was in the hands of others. North Africa was an Italian theatre and German forces were there at the behest of Mussolini to help defeat their common enemy Britain. Chief of Staff of the Italian Army, **Maresciallo Ugo Cavallero (1880–1943)**, was the Commando Supremo who reported directly to Benito Mussolini. He was the former C-in-C East Africa before he was called back to Rome to succeed Maresciallo (Marshal) Badoglio. Reporting to Cavallero as C-in-C North Africa was **Maresciallo Ettore Bastico (1876–1972)**. Bastico was in fact Rommel's immediate commander in the field as he was the overall leader of all Italian and German forces. In reality, Rommel reported directly to his boss, **Generalfeldmarschall Albert Kesselring**, C-in-C Mediterranean, in charge of all German forces in the region reporting directly to Berlin. Rommel was frustrated by this convoluted chain of command which meant that all the crucial supply decisions to Axis forces in North Africa were under Italian control, as were all shipping and transport.

The cutting edge of Panzerarmee Afrika was mainly provided by the Afrika Korps under the command of **Generalleutnant Walther Nehring (1892–1983)**. He took over command of the famed Panzer force on 9 March 1942. Its previous commander, Ludwig Crüwell, had been moved by Rommel to organize and lead a group of two Italian corps, labelled Gruppe Crüwell, for the coming attack on the Gazala Line.

Nehring was an infantry veteran of World War I who later joined the great armoured commander Guderian to help form the new Panzer arm of the German Army. At the start of World War II, Nehring was Chief of Staff of XIX Korps. In October 1941 he was given command of 18.Panzer Division in Russia where he fought with distinction. Further promotion brought him to North Africa and command of the Afrika Korps.

Generaloberst Erwin Rommel, Commander Panzerarmee Afrika, the charismatic opponent of the British in North Africa. Three times the Panzer leader overwhelmed British Eighth Army and twice extricated his forces from almost overwhelming defeats. (IWM, GER 1281)

A forlorn General der Panzertruppe Ludwig Crüwell, Commander Gruppe Crüwell, walks away from a British headquarters and into captivity. Crüwell was shot down whilst flying over 50th Division's positions in the Gazala Line. (IWM, E12661)

Rommel (left) in conference with the commander of the Afrika Korps, Generalleutnant Walther Nehring. (IWM, HU6510))

General der Panzertruppe Ludwig Crüwell had earlier commanded the 2.Infanterie Division (mot) in France in 1940, fighting alongside Rommel's 7.Panzer Division. He had served in World War I in a cavalry regiment and remained with mechanized forces as the German Panzer arm of the Wehrmacht took shape. He then fought in Poland and Russia where he won admiration for his brave and skilful handling of armoured forces. By the end of 1941 he had been awarded the oak leaves to the Knight's Cross he had won in Russia and had been promoted to General der Panzertruppe. He was an obvious choice to take over command of the Afrika Korps when Rommel's forces were expanded to Panzergruppe status in August 1941. During the latter stages of the *Crusader* battles, Crüwell suffered from jaundice and returned home on sick leave. Walther Nehring took his place at the head of the Afrika Korps. Crüwell arrived back in North Africa just before the start of the Gazala offensive and was given command of the Italian infantry divisions to the north of the line.

With seasoned armoured commanders at army and corps level, it is not surprising that Rommel's divisional commanders were also specialized in tank and mobile warfare. **Generalmajor Georg von Bismarck**, commander 21.Panzer Division, was well known to Rommel for he was a regimental commander in his 7.Panzer Division during the campaign in the Low Countries in 1940. Bismarck's Schützen Regiment 7 took part in the drive through France and Belgium and succeeded in helping to cut off British and French forces at St Valéry and Cherbourg. **Generalmajor Gustav von Vaerst**, commander of 15.Panzer Division, was also a veteran of the lightning war of 1940 in France and the Low Countries. **Generalmajor Ulrich Kleeman** who led 90.leichte Division had seen active service with 3.Schützen-Brigade in France and Russia.

The two mobile Italian divisions, the 'Ariete' armoured and the 'Trieste' motorized divisions, were also led by men with experience of mobile warfare. **Generale di Divisione Giuseppe de Stephanis (1885–1965)** had previously commanded an armoured artillery corps and the 102ª Divisione Infanteria (infantry division) 'Trento' before taking over the 132ª Divisione Corazzata (armoured division) 'Ariete'. **Generale di Divisione Francesco La Ferla**, had led the 101ª Divisione Motorizzate (motorized division) 'Trieste' since the previous year during the *Crusader* battles.

Generale di Corpo d'Armata Benvenuto Gioda commanded Italian X Corpo as part of Gruppe Crüwell. During Mussolini's rise to power he had led V MSVN Divisione (blackshirt division) and had served in Ethiopia. In 1940, after Italy had declared war on France, he was part of the army of occupation in command of the Italian 4ª Divisione 'Livorno'. **Generale di Corpo d'Armata Enea Navarini** was one of the few Italian generals that Rommel respected; he called him his 'trusted friend'. Navarini had previously commanded the Italian 56ª Divisione 'Casale' in Greece before arriving in North Africa in 1941 to head the Italian XXI Corpo comprising the Sabratha and Trento divisions.

OPPOSING ARMIES

The British retreat into the Gazala Line and the rapidity of Rommel's eastward advance had once more demonstrated the inferior quality of the British forces and tactics compared with the Germans. Training, organization and equipment were again found to be inadequate when facing Rommel's desert veterans. The morale of British troops was falling as they began to lose confidence in their weapons and, to some extent, in their commanders. But things were about to change, for a long period of static holding of the line followed the withdrawal while Eighth Army readied itself for its coming offensive, and this respite enabled some of these failures to be addressed.

BRITISH FORCES

In the months that followed the retreat the situation started to improve as new weapons began to arrive in the theatre. British troops were well aware of the disparity between British and German arms. The two main disadvantages that Eighth Army faced were with the two principal weapons it had at its disposal with which to counter German tanks: the 2-pdr (40mm) anti-tank gun and the Crusader tank. The small shell fired by the 2-pdr gun just did not have the

Stuart light tanks of the 8th King's Royal Irish Hussars advance at speed across the desert. The light tanks were thinly armoured and very vulnerable to enemy anti-tank fire. They were used primarily in a reconnaissance role. (IWM, E5065)

stopping power that was required to damage German armour at anywhere near the distance that tank versus gun actions should take place, while the Crusader's mechanical unreliability and the poor penetrating power of its main weapon put British armour at a distinct disadvantage.

The 2-pdr anti-tank gun was, fortunately, being replaced by the more potent 6-pdr gun, although only 112 of these new weapons arrived before the start of the battle, and a new American tank, the Grant, was being made available in enough quantities to allow at least one squadron of them to be allocated to each armoured regiment. The Grant was equipped with a greater thickness of defensive armour than the Crusader and was much more reliable mechanically than any British tank. Its main armament was a 75mm gun capable of firing both anti-tank and high explosive rounds. It was more than a match for any of the enemy's anti-tank guns or tanks, with the exception of the deadly 88mm anti-aircraft weapon that the Germans used in the desert in the anti-tank role. The Grant did, however, have a major drawback, for its main weapon was housed in a fixed sponson on the side of the vehicle which limited its ability to traverse, but there was some compensation to be had from the additional 37mm gun that it housed in its turret.

Of the other tanks in Eighth Army, the infantry tanks of the two army tank brigades were obsolescent Maltidas and newer Valentines. Although these tanks were more heavily armoured than the cruiser tanks, they were slow to manoeuvre and had a poor main weapon. The standard light tank used for reconnaissance and observation work was the American-built Stuart. It was armed with a 37mm gun and was able to fire anti-tank capped armour-piercing ammunition.

One of the main lessons gathered from the *Crusader* battle was the effectiveness and flexibility of Rommel's Panzer divisions. Auchinleck therefore decided that changes had to be made to British tank formations to give his forces a more adaptable approach to armoured warfare. He believed that the various arms that comprised an armoured division needed to be better integrated. He reasoned that the British type of armoured division

would be more balanced if it too had less armour and more infantry like those of the Afrika Korps.

On 11 February the basic organization of armoured divisions in the Middle East was changed to make the 'brigade group' the basic battle formation. One of the two armoured brigades in the armoured division was to be replaced by a motorized infantry brigade. Both of these brigades now became 'brigade groups' after the addition of units taken from the old support groups, which were now abolished. Instead of having anti-tank, anti-aircraft and field artillery held separately within the division, these would now be incorporated into each brigade along with engineer and administrative units. Tanks would go into battle with supporting artillery and anti-tank units up with them just like the Germans. At least, that was the idea, as was Auchinleck's decree that armour had to be kept concentrated and not split into 'penny packets' all over the battlefield. Unfortunately, once battle had been joined, some of these ideas often went the way of many other good intentions.

The net result in numbers of tanks of this reorganization of armoured forces was as follows: 1st and 7th armoured divisions could muster 167 Grants, 149 Stuarts and 257 Crusaders; 1st and 32nd army tank brigades together had 166 Valentines and 110 Matildas and the 1st Armoured Brigade, which was to join in the battle at a later stage, had 75 Grants and 70 Stuarts. This gave a complete total, including reserves, of 994 tanks.

Lieutenant-General Ritchie had two corps under command at the start of the battle of Gazala, Lt. Gen. Gott's XIII Corps and Lt. Gen. Norrie's XXX Corps. The bulk of the infantry was with Gott and consisted of the 50th and the 1st and 2nd South African divisions. Armoured support was available from 1st and 32nd army tank brigades. Norrie's corps consisted of the 1st and 7th armoured divisions both of which had been enlarged by the addition of other formations: the 1st with an extra armoured brigade group and the 7th with two extra motor infantry brigades and a motor brigade group. Under army command as a reserve was the 5th Indian Division, with further reserves on call from Iraq (10th Indian Division) and Egypt (11th Indian Brigade and

New to the desert in time for action at Gazala were the 6-pdr anti-tank guns. Here one is shown being fired by an Australian crew during a training session in Egypt. (IWM, E14386)

1st Armoured Brigade). The standard infantry division at that time consisted of three brigades each with three rifle battalions, a reconnaissance regiment of armoured cars, a machine-gun battalion and three field and one anti-tank regiments of artillery.

Air Vice-Marshal Sir Arthur Coningham's Desert Air Force provided air support for Eighth Army. Numerically it was inferior to the enemy, only able to put 190 serviceable aircraft into the air as opposed to the 497 serviceable aircraft available to the Germans and Italians. For most of the battle the RAF contested air space with units of the Luftwaffe and the Italian Regia Aeronautica without either side completely gaining the upper hand. Once the battle began it was difficult for the Desert Air Force to aid Eighth Army with direct support because of the fluid and confused nature of the fighting. Its contribution to the action was more the bombing of supply lines and the chasing away of enemy aircraft. Things became worse during the later stage of the battle as the enemy advanced and threatened to overrun landing grounds, which led to RAF units withdrawing to airfields farther to the east.

Both the British and the Axis forces had long supply lines stretching back across the desert. Tobruk was a supply port for Eighth Army, but little was being landed there because of the close proximity to the enemy. Virtually everything that Ritchie required for the forthcoming offensive had to be brought forward the 400km from Egypt by lorry or train. Two large supply dumps were set up ready for the planned attack, one in Tobruk and the other just north of El Adem at Belhamed. Both of them were near enough to the front line to be useful for the attack, but their presence so close to the fighting meant that they could prove a liability if anything went wrong.

AXIS FORCES

At the start of Rommel's campaign at Gazala, his troops were in fine spirit. Their advance from El Agheila and the rapid withdrawal of Eighth Army before them had given them great heart. Now, at the end of May, after a period of rest, replenishment and re-training they were even more eager for battle. Rommel was once more on the offensive and his whole force was confident that this time the British would be driven from North Africa.

Like the British, the Germans were receiving new weapons before the battle. The most important of these was a new model of the Panzerkampfwagen (PzKpfw) III tank, the 'Mark III Special'. It was armed with a long 5cm gun similar to the successful Pak 38 anti-tank gun. The extra length of the barrel produced greater muzzle velocity and therefore greater penetrating power. By the time of the Gazala offensive these tanks were starting to arrive, although only 19 of them actually took part in the opening stages of the battle. Since the start of 1942 all German tanks delivered to North Africa enjoyed the standard provision of face-hardened armour, which cut down even further the effectiveness of British anti-tank ammunition.

The newer PzKpfw IV tank was also arriving in the theatre in growing numbers but still constituted a small part of the overall tank force. At the start of the battle the Afrika Korps contained 332 tanks, of which 50 were PzKpfw IIs, 242 PzKpfw IIIs (including 19 'Specials') and 40 PzKpfw IVs,

with 77 tanks of various marks in reserve. The Italian main tanks were the M13/40 and the M14/41 variant, neither of which was a great threat to the British. In terms of armament, protection and performance they remained the poorest of all the armour in the desert.

The German armoured divisions comprised one Panzer and one motorized infantry regiment; the Italian 132ᵃ Divisione Corazzata 'Ariete' was similarly configured, containing one tank regiment and one motorized infantry regiment. The 90.leichte Division, previously titled the Afrika Division, contained three motorized infantry regiments. The Italian 101ᵃ Divisione Motorizzate 'Trieste' and all Italian infantry divisions contained just two infantry regiments.

Outclassing every other weapon on the battlefield with the flat trajectory of its high-velocity shells was the German 88mm gun. Strictly speaking the gun was an anti-aircraft weapon, but it was being increasingly used in an anti-tank role and its effects were devastating. Whenever British tanks came up against this weapon they took tremendous losses as the gun was able to engage them at distances from which they could not retaliate. Even the

standard German anti-tank gun, the 5cm Pak 38, was more than a match for any of Eighth Army's tanks. Fortunately, the British had little to fear from the Italian Army's main anti-tank gun, the 47/32 M35 model, for it had even less penetrative power than their own 2-pdr anti-tank weapon.

Erwin Rommel was a commander who had supreme confidence in his own ability and in the German troops under his command. His subordinate commanders were among the best that Germany had available; all were well versed in mobile warfare and each of them understood Rommel's approach to battle. Rommel was not an easy commander to work for, he drove his men hard, was often absent from his headquarters and was invariably up with his leading units out of touch with the rest of the battlefield driving the tanks forwards. He had a low opinion of British commanders, but nonetheless entertained a great respect for the bravery and doggedness of British troops. Rommel was sure that his German mobile formations would win the battle by staying mobile and striking the British armour with maximum force, whilst his Italian divisions tied down the British infantry.

ORDERS OF BATTLE

BRITISH FORCES

Commander-in-Chief Middle East – Gen. Claude Auchinleck
Eighth Army – Lt. Gen. Neil Ritchie

XIII CORPS – LT. GEN. W. GOTT

50th Division – Maj. Gen. W. Ramsden
  69th Brigade Group
  150th Brigade Group
  151st Brigade Group

1st South African Division – Maj. Gen. D. Pienaar
  1st South African Brigade Group

2nd South African Brigade Group
3rd South African Brigade Group

2nd South African Division – Maj. Gen. H. Klopper
  4th South African Brigade Group
  6th South African Brigade Group
  9th Indian Brigade Group

1st Army Tank Brigade
32nd Army Tank Brigade

XXX CORPS – LT. GEN. NORRIE

1st Armoured Division – Maj. Gen. H. Lumsden
   2nd Armoured Brigade Group
   22nd Armoured Brigade Group
   201st Guards (Motor) Brigade

7th Armoured Division – Maj. Gen. F. Messervy
   4th Armoured Brigade Group
   7th Motor Brigade Group
   3rd Indian Motor Brigade Group
   29th Indian Brigade Group

1ère Brigade Française Libre

Under Army command:
5th Indian Division – Maj. Gen. H. Briggs
   10th Indian Brigade Group
2e Brigade Française Libre

Later joined Army command:
10th Indian Division – Maj. Gen. T. Rees
   20th Indian Brigade
   21st Indian Brigade
   25th Indian Brigade
11th Indian Infantry Brigade
1st Armoured Brigade

AXIS FORCES

Commander-in-Chief Armed Forces North Africa –
Maresciallo E. Bastico
Panzerarmee Afrika – Gen. der Pz. E. Rommel

GRUPPE CRÜWELL– GEN. DER PZ. L. CRÜWELL

Italian X Corpo – Gen. di corpo Benvenuto Gioda
27ª Divisione 'Brescia' – Gen. di Div. G. Lombardi
   19° Reggimento di Fanteria
   20° Reggimento di Fanteria
   1° Reggimento di Fanteria

17ª Divisione 'Pavia' – Gen. di Div. A. Torriano
   27° Reggimento di Fanteria
   28° Reggimento di Fanteria
   26° Reggimento di Artiglieria

Italian XXI Corpo – Gen. di Corpo d'Armata E. Navarini
60ª Divisione 'Sabratha' – Gen. di Div. M. Soldarelli
   85° Reggimento di Fanteria
   86° Reggimento di Fanteria
   42ª Reggimento di Artiglieria

102ª Divisione 'Trento' – Gen. di Div. F. Scotti
   61° Reggimento Fanteria Motorizzata
   62° Reggimento Fanteria Motorizzata
   7° Reggimento Bersaglieri Motorizzato
   46° Reggimento Artiglieria Motorizzato

15.Schützen Brigade (mot)
Gruppe Hecker

GRUPPE ROMMEL – GEN. DER PZ. ERWIN ROMMEL

Deutsches Afrika Korps - Gen.Lt. W. Nehring
15.Panzer Division – Gen.Maj. G. von Vaerst
   Panzer Regiment 8
   Schützen Regiment 115 (mot)
   Artillerie Regiment 33 (mot)

21.Panzer Division – Gen.Maj. G. von Bismarck
   Panzer Regiment 5
   Schützen Regiment 104 (mot)
   Artillerie Regiment 105 (mot)

90.leichte Division – Gen.Maj. U. Kleeman
   leichte Infanterie Regiment 155
   leichte Infanterie Regiment 200
   leichte Infanterie Regiment 361
   Artillerie Regiment 190

Italian XX Corpo d'Armata –
Gen. di Corpo d'armata Ettore Baldassare
132ª Divisione Corazzata 'Ariete' –
Gen. di Corpo d'Armata G. de Stephanis
   132ª Reggimento Carri M (medium)
   32ª Reggimento Carri L (light)
   8ª Reggimento Bersaglieri Motorizzato
   132ª Reggimento Artiglieria Motorizzato

101ª Divisione Motorizzate 'Trieste' – Gen. di Div. F. La Ferla
   65ª Reggimento Fanteria Motorizzata
   66ª Reggimento Fanteria Motorizzata
   9ª Reggimento Bersaglieri Motorizzato
   21ª Reggimento Artiglieria Motorizzato

OPPOSING PLANS

BRITISH PLANS

After Eighth Army had been driven back into the relative security of the Gazala–Bir Hacheim Line, Ritchie set about consolidating his defences and preparing to resume his advance westwards. Meanwhile, Auchinleck was dealing with an irate Winston Churchill, who was appalled at the setbacks and was urging his Commander-in-Chief to get back on the offensive. The war was going badly for Britain and the country was desperate for some sort of victory.

Fortunately, things were gradually improving in the British camp for reinforcements and extra formations were arriving in the theatre in greater numbers. Auchinleck's main concern was assembling enough armour with which to counter the enemy. He stated that he would need 3:2 superiority in tanks over the Axis to ensure success in the attack and he calculated that by the end of April he would be ready to take on Rommel once again. However, before this offensive could be undertaken, much organization and training needed to be done to bring Eighth Army up to scratch. Auchinleck did not envisage going over to the offensive before 1 June. This somewhat pacified the

General Auchinleck (standing) and other senior officers watch a newly arrived Grant tank demonstrate the accuracy and power of its sponson-mounted main 75mm gun. (IWM, E8458)

A squadron of Grants from one of Eighth Army's armoured regiments sweep across the desert in battle order on the 8 June 1942 during an attack on the Cauldron. (IWM, E13017)

Prime Minister, although Churchill continually urged Auchinleck to regain the initiative in the desert as soon as he could so that some assistance could be given to the besieged and battered island of Malta.

The position held by Eighth Army after its flight from the borders of Tripolitania back into Cyrenaica ran from Gazala near the coast down to Bir Hacheim located well into the desolate sandy wastes of the desert in the south. It consisted of a series of brigade-sized defensive 'boxes' surrounded by wire, mines and trenches with an occasional bunker sited to cover the approaches. These boxes were linked together with extensive minefields and obstacles, although they were too widely spaced to be mutually supporting or to have the whole of these minefields covered by artillery fire. The line blocked all routes eastwards, including the metalled road along the coast, the Via Balbia, the tracks west of Acroma and the two desert routes along the Trig Capuzzo and the Trig el Abd. Two rear positions were also constructed, one defending Acroma and the other, labelled 'Knightsbridge', around the junction of a track leading south from Acroma and the Trig Capuzzo. Auchinleck ordered that the Gazala Line be held in strength whilst Tobruk was built up as a base for the forthcoming offensive.

If Rommel attacked, Tobruk was to be held if possible but Auchinleck did not intend to allow a British force to be besieged there again. If the enemy ever got to a position whereby it looked as though the port would be encircled, the garrison was to be evacuated and withdrawn with the rest of Eighth Army back to the frontier of Egypt. Tobruk was never again to be used as an isolated thorn in the enemy's rear for propaganda purposes.

Legionnaires from Gén. de brig. Koenig's garrison at Bir Hacheim training in the desert. (IWM, 13313)

By the beginning of May British intelligence reports suggested that Rommel would be ready to launch his attack against Eighth Army before Auchinleck was ready to renew his offensive. Eighth Army's commander was therefore instructed to prepare for this eventuality whilst still planning for his renewed advance westwards. Ritchie had to decide whether to concentrate his forces and risk Rommel bypassing them with an outflanking movement, or to extend the front to its limits forcing the enemy into a wide sweep into the southern desert. This latter option would increase the length of his supply route and leave it vulnerable to a strike by Eighth Army from the north. He decided, with Auchinleck's agreement, to go for the extended line option and considered that an overall weakening of the front would be compensated for by the extra difficulties it would place on Rommel if he tried an outflanking attack.

Although Ritchie was the actual army commander in the field, Auchinleck continued to try to influence his tactics. He suggested that all of Ritchie's armour should be concentrated in XXX Corps and held astride the Trig Capuzzo to the east of El Adem. From this position it could move against a break-in on the centre of the line or against a sweep around the southern flank. Auchinleck stressed that the armoured divisions should fight as complete formations under the control of XXX Corp's commander and not be sent into battle piecemeal to be used as stopgaps.

Eighth Army held its positions with Lt. Gen. Gott's XIII Corps along the line in the north from the junction with the coast down to just below Knightsbridge on the Trig Capuzzo. To the south the line consisted of an extensive minefield that then linked into the positions around Bir Hacheim held by the 1ère Brigade Française Libre, which came under the command of XXX Corps. The bulk of XXX Corps with all the armour was positioned in the rear south of the Trig Capuzzo. General Ritchie was of the opinion that the main threat was more likely to be made in the south and therefore positioned his armour much farther to the south than Auchinleck would have wished.

RIGHT
A small Volkswagen Kübelwagen is dwarfed by a passing SdKfz 7 half-track. The licence plate of the Kübelwagen shows that it belongs to the Feldpost and its driver is probably delivering letters from home to the desert troops. The half-track is being used by a Luftwaffe gun crew as the prime mover for the 88mm Flak gun they have in tow. (IWM, MH5830)

BELOW
A well-camouflaged German forward artillery observer post close to the British lines before the start of the Gazala battle. (IWM, MH5877)

AXIS PLANS

After the impressive gains made by Rommel's attack in January, Mussolini made it clear to him that his prime responsibility was the defence of Tripolitania. No further supplies could be got to him for some time and so he was ordered to hold the British along their defence line and make no further moves eastwards until he had reorganized and replenished his forces. It was clear that the British were in no fit state to resume any offensive for at least six weeks. In the meantime, Rommel was to gather strength to be ready to repulse this attack when it came.

On 1 May Hitler met with Mussolini at Berchtesgaden to discuss the Mediterranean campaign. Supplies to their forces in North Africa were being hampered by attacks on Axis convoys by British forces in Malta. The resistance from the island had to be eliminated. The Führer and the Duce agreed on a plan – Operation *Herkules* – for an invasion of Malta to be made by the Italians supported by a German parachute division. But first, the

British airfields around Gazala had to be captured to prevent the RAF interfering with the attack. The two leaders therefore gave the go-ahead for Operation *Aida*, a drive to the Nile that would begin towards the end of May to forestall the expected British offensive. The first phase of this drive would be the defeat of Eighth Army at Gazala, the capture of Tobruk and the elimination of British forces up to the Egyptian border. At this point Operation *Herkules* would take place, Malta would be captured and the Mediterranean Sea opened for Axis convoys to land supplies into Benghazi and Tobruk. Rommel's forces would then be replenished over secure supply lines with sufficient reinforcements, fuel and ammunition to continue the drive eastwards through Egypt and over the Nile.

A German 88mm gun in action. The dual-purpose anti-aircraft/anti-tank gun had a formidable reputation in the desert and was more than a match for any tank that was deployed in the theatre, able to engage British tanks at ranges greater than they were able to reply. (IWM, MH5853)

Shortly after his meeting with Mussolini, Hitler had doubts about the Duce's forces carrying out the invasion of Malta. He summed up his misgivings a few days later: the Italians could never keep anything secret; they did not have the fighting spirit to undertake the difficult task of an amphibious landing; they almost certainly would not arrive in time to assist the German paratroops and their navy would not dare face the Royal Navy. The end result could be German troops being stranded without supplies after the airborne assault. Hitler therefore ordered that preparations for Operation *Herkules* and the capture of Malta should proceed only on paper and be abandoned if Rommel succeeded in taking the port of Tobruk.

Rommel was pleased with the outcome of the Führer's meeting at Berchtesgaden. He had at last been given permission to go flat out for victory. He had been promised a free hand and sufficient supplies to drive the British out of North Africa. No more would he have to make partial moves and then seek permission to develop his success. Rommel could now make plans without someone looking over his shoulder ready to rein him in.

Rommel intended that Ritchie's army be misled into expecting the main attack to be in the north and centre of the Gazala Line, hoping that the British would then deploy their armour behind the infantry positions in that sector. He would create this diversionary attack whilst his actual main thrust would be made in the south round the Bir Hacheim position. Even if the British command did not wholly fall for this ruse, they should at least send some of their armour to counter the attempted break-in in the north, thus splitting the strike power they had available to move against the southern attack.

Rommel decided that Gruppe Crüwell would make a subsidiary move in the afternoon of 26 May against the positions held by the British 50th Division and the 1st South African Division between the Trig Capuzzo and the coast, whilst he made the main assault with the bulk of his armour and mobile forces in the south. For the attack, Crüwell would have under command Italian X and XXI corps supported by most of Rommel's artillery and a German infantry brigade. Also available to him for the initial move would be two regiments of armour, one from Italian XX Corpo and one from the Afrika Korps. They were to be under command for the first few hours of Crüwell's advance, just long enough for the British to identify that an armoured attack was under way. This tank force would then be withdrawn and motor south to join the remainder of the Panzer regiments for Rommel's main assault. Whilst Crüwell was pushing into the centre of the British line, Rommel would personally lead the Afrika Korps, the 90.leichte Division and the Italian XX Corpo under the cover of darkness around Bir Hacheim ready to drive north at dawn towards Acroma to get behind the British XIII Corps. Gott's corps would then be attacked from both the east and the west. At this point the Gruppe Hecker would make an amphibious landing between Gazala and Tobruk to cut communications linking British XIII Corps and Tobruk. The 90.leichte Division would move farther to the east towards El Adem and the British supply centre at Belhamed.

THE GAZALA CAMPAIGN

A flight of Ju 87 Stuka dive-bombers on their way to attack one of Eighth Army's positions. The Stuka's ability to bomb areas with great accuracy led them to become an important weapon in Rommel's arsenal, where they were almost considered as being long-range artillery. (IWM, MH 5591)

PHASE ONE: ROMMEL ATTACKS

In the late afternoon of 26 May, Gruppe Crüwell began to move slowly towards the centre of the British positions between Gazala and Sidi Muftah. Overhead the shells of the supporting artillery barrage screamed towards the dug-in positions of British XIII Corps, whilst Stukas bombed and strafed the defences of the Gazala Line. The advance threw up great columns of smoke and dust, which both obscured Crüwell's movements and also gave the impression to the waiting British that this was the start of Rommel's offensive. This belief was further reinforced when reconnaissance aircraft picked up the armoured feint moving towards the centre of Eighth Army's line. The tanks sent a great pall of sand and dust billowing up into the sky, then, just as the light began to fade, the Panzers were replaced by trucks carrying aircraft engines which slowly circled around churning up yet more dust to prolong the sense of gathering armour. Meanwhile, the tanks pulled back and headed south to join Gruppe Rommel.

By the time that dusk had fallen, Panzerarmee Afrika with Rommel at its head was moving to the south-east towards Bir Hacheim. Rommel was hoping that his advance would achieve complete surprise, but armoured cars from the 4th South African Armoured Car Regiment were observing and shadowing his motorized columns from a discrete distance, reporting all movements back to corps HQ. During the hours of darkness the German armoured force stopped to refuel. Just before dawn, with his men fed and rested, Rommel prepared his commanders for the commencement of battle.

At around 0430hrs this vast motorized force moved out into the desert. On the left was Gen. Baldassare's Italian XX Corpo with its 228 tanks, in the centre was Gen.Lt. Nehring's Afrika Korps with the 332 Panzers in its two divisions, with Gen.Maj. von Bismarck's 21.Panzer Division on the left and Gen.Maj. von Vaerst's 15.Panzer Division on the right. On the extreme right wing was the 90.leichte Division, beginning its long drive up to El Adem and the British main supply dump at Belhamed. The Afrika Korps moved forwards in battle formation. At the head of each division were its tanks, with engineers, artillery and signals tucked in behind. In the centre of the formation were the trucks carrying the infantry, flanked on either side by anti-tank guns. To the rear, protected by the offensive arms of the division, were the thousands of vehicles of the supply echelons, each laden down with extra fuel, ammunition and rations.

Rommel's attack on the Gazala Line

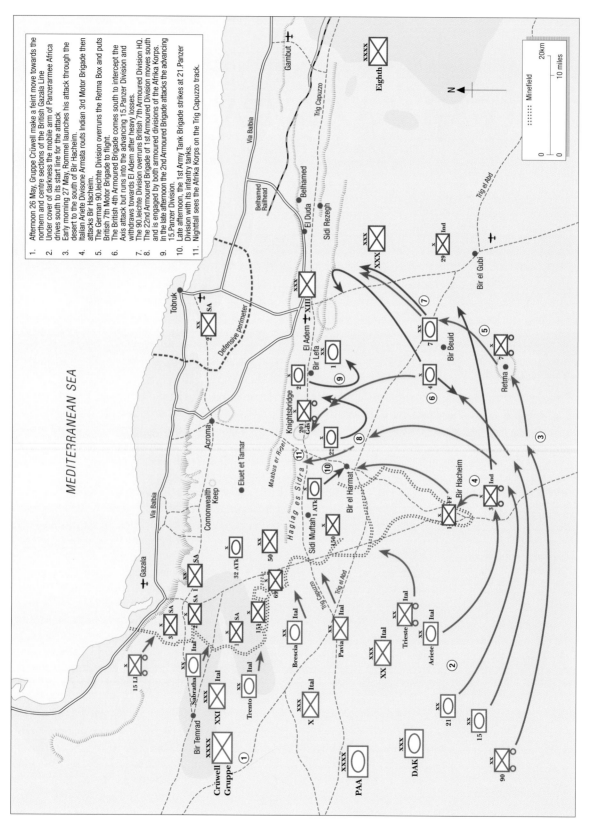

1. Afternoon 26 May, Gruppe Crüwell make a feint move towards the northern and centre sections of the British Gazala Line
2. Under cover of darkness the mobile arm of Panzerarmee Africa drives south to its start line for the attack
3. Early morning 27 May, Rommel launches his attack through the desert to the south of Bir Hacheim.
4. Italian Ariete Divisone Armata routs Indian 3rd Motor Brigade then attacks Bir Hacheim.
5. The German 90.leichte Division overruns the Retma Box and puts British 7th Motor Brigade to flight.
6. The British 4th Armoured Brigade comes south to intercept the Axis attack but runs into the advancing 15.Panzer Division and withdraws towards El Adem after heavy losses.
7. The 90.leichte Division overruns British 7th Armoured Division HQ.
8. The 22nd Armoured Brigade of 1st Armoured Division moves south and is engaged by both armoured divisions of the Afrika Korps.
9. In the late afternoon the 2nd Armoured Brigade attacks the advancing 15.Panzer Division.
10. Late afternoon, the 1st Army Tank Brigade strikes at 21.Panzer Division with its infantry tanks.
11. Nightfall sees the Afrika Korps on the Trig Capuzzo track.

MEDITERRANEAN SEA

20km

10 miles

N

::::::: Minefield

South African troops in infantry positions along the Gazala Line watch from their trench as a nearby position comes under attack. (IWM, E12296)

South of Bir Hacheim Rommel began to execute a left wheel to bring his army northwards towards the centre rear of Eighth Army. Bir Hacheim itself and the Free French who garrisoned the outpost were left for the 132ᵃ Divisione Corazzata 'Ariete' to deal with. As Rommel motored out into the vast wastes of the desert his spirits were high. He felt sure that his movements had been unobserved and that he could now fall on the rear of the British with devastating effect. All appeared to be going to plan.

In the British camp Ritchie and Norrie had been given news of Rommel's moves throughout the night, but they could not decide whether the activity south of Bir Hacheim was the feint that everyone had predicted and that the main attack was being made by Gruppe Crüwell in the north. This uncertainty led to few concrete decisions, although at 0230hrs the 4th Armoured Brigade was told to move at first light to its battle position 14km to the south, where it would be able to support both the 3rd Indian Motor Brigade and the 7th Motor Brigade. Things became much clearer at around 0630hrs when Brigadier Filose, commander of the newly arrived 3rd Indian Motor Brigade, reported to Maj. Gen. Messervy at 7th Armoured Division's HQ that he faced 'a whole bloody German armoured division'.

The brigade, then just south of Bir Hacheim, was in fact being attacked by the 132ᵃ Divisione Corazzata 'Ariete' and the Italians were in almost the same state of shock as the Indians for they were oblivious to the motor brigade's existence across their line of advance. Reacting quickly, the armour of the Italian division tore into the hastily prepared defences of the motor brigade and within 30 minutes had virtually wiped out the whole of Brig. Filose's command. Those units and individuals that could extricate themselves fell back to the north and east, leaving over 450 officers and men of the brigade in the hands of the Italians as prisoners of war.

Defenders of the Bir Hacheim Box from the 13e Demi-Brigade de Légion Étrangère tuck in to British rations eaten straight from the tin. The legionnaire on the left is attempting to enjoy one of the mainstays of British army food, a tin of 'bully beef'. (IWM, E8397)

The Italians were elated by their success but soon came down to earth when they realised that it was not in fact the Bir Hacheim locality that they had eliminated as ordered, but a separate defensive position the location of which was unknown to Rommel. Nonetheless, the 132ª Divisione Corazzata 'Ariete' had achieved a notable victory and the morale of its troops soared as they headed north towards the French enclave above which the Stukas were already circling.

Over to the east, on the right of Rommel's group, the 90.leichte Division had also made contact with an outpost of Eighth Army. Its leading units had run into patrols from the 7th Motor Brigade with some surprise, for it was another formation that Rommel had been oblivious to. The British turned and fled back into the brigade's defensive box around Retma, hotly pursued by Gen.Maj. Kleeman's motorized infantry. The speed and strength of the German advance slammed into the Retma Box and rolled over the hastily prepared British positions in quick order, once again putting the defenders to flight, sending them streaming back north-eastwards towards Bir el Gubi.

By this time the 4th Armoured Brigade was moving southwards oblivious to the fact that Rommel's army was heading straight for it. In the lead was the 3rd Royal Tank Regiment (3rd RTR). The battalion's troops had had time to breakfast before they moved out at 0730hrs and in a short space of time ran headlong into the advancing tanks of 15.Panzer Division. Fortunately they were deployed for action and the Grants opened fire on the advancing Germans with startling effect. The Germans were taken by complete surprise. In the words of Rommel: 'The advent of the new American tank tore great holes in our ranks. Our entire force now stood in heavy and destructive combat with a superior enemy.' The fury of the fire temporarily brought 15.Panzer Division to a halt.

As the large silhouette of the Grants loomed up out of the haze and dust there was some panic in the German lines. Some spoke of a rout as the British advanced into the columns of vehicles. Soft-top transports wheeled around and drove to the rear, tanks were firing in all directions and some order was lost. Generalmajor von Vaerst rallied his men then sent a battalion of tanks round to the right to surprise the British, supporting this move with a battery of 88mm guns. The flanks of 3rd RTR, spread out across the desert, caught the force of this counterattack and they lost a number of tanks in quick succession. It soon became clear to the battalion that a force much larger than first supposed opposed it, and so it retired hastily to the north.

The 8th Hussars were behind 3rd RTR and they were not so fortunate as to be able to withdraw, for Vaerst's Panzers hit them before they had time to deploy. This sudden clash of armour virtually wiped them out. The 4th Armoured Brigade's other tank battalion, 5th RTR, was six kilometres farther north and was just moving off when it had the misfortune to become engaged with Gen.Maj. von Bismarck's 21.Panzer Division as it was driving past its right flank. Once again the shock of meeting a whole Panzer division led to a fierce firefight and a heavy toll of men and equipment destroyed and captured. All three of these British tank battalions from 4th Armoured Brigade took great losses from these encounters before the survivors could extricate themselves and retire to the north-east to regroup. Hard pressed by marauding Panzers they fell back 32km to the north-east to the El Adem area. They had, however, given Rommel a sharp shock and knocked out a great number of his tank force. It was not the immediate start that the German army commander had wanted.

Meanwhile 90.leichte Division continued on its push northwards towards El Adem. Kleeman's motorized infantry had overrun the 7th Motor Brigade's positions with such speed that the desert ahead of them was full of British transport of all kinds fleeing in some disorder. At British 7th Armoured Division's HQ, just 13km north-east of the Retma Box, Maj. Gen. Messervy had been listening with some discomfort to messages coming in that both of his brigades were in serious trouble. Messervy did not appreciate just how quickly the enemy was moving towards him until, at around 0845hrs, he was surprised to learn that German armoured cars were bearing down on his advance HQ.

The divisional staff moved their armoured command vehicles (ACVs) three kilometres to the north-east, but even there things were still frantic. Shells and bullets seemed to be coming at them from all directions and there was so much dust and smoke that it was difficult to see what was happening. The five ACVs that made up the headquarters became separated and then found themselves mixed up with German armoured cars. Three of the command vehicles made off to the north, but two others were immobilized and captured. Unfortunately one of these ACVs contained the commanding officer and his staff. Major-General Messervy, his brigadier RA and his chief of staff were all taken prisoner. The general had had just enough time to remove his badges of rank and he went into captivity as a private soldier, mixed in with the rest of his team. In just a few short hours virtually the whole of the 7th Armoured Division had been routed, dispersed across the desert and left leaderless. Messervy was, however, able to slip away from his captors and get back to his division two days later.

With one of his armoured divisions now completely out of action XXX Corps' commander had to act swiftly. Lieutenant-General Norrie had

A broken-down or possibly damaged Crusader tank is recovered from the desert and loaded onto a tank transporter to be ferried back to a maintenance centre for refurbishment and subsequent return to battle. (IWM, E13080)

A BRITISH HURRICANE FIGHTER FROM THE DESERT AIR FORCE ATTACKS A CONVOY ATTEMPTING TO GET SUPPLIES FORWARD TO THE GERMAN AFRIKA KORPS DURING THE OPENING DAYS OF ROMMEL'S GAZALA OFFENSIVE (pp. 38–39)

The Libyan Desert was extremely inhospitable terrain over which to wage war (**1**). By the month of June, when the Gazala battles were in full spate, temperatures were beginning to reach their maximum, sandstorms were common and the glare of the sun blinded those who tried to see through its permanent shimmering heat haze. All supplies, the most vital of which were ammunition, fuel and water, had to be transported across barren wasteland in quantities that taxed the endurance of the most capable of logistical organizations. Most transportation was carried out by wheeled vehicles and the shifting areas of soft sand and shallow depressions meant that supply columns were forced to stick to the more compacted ground which marked out known Bedouin tracks and primitive roadways (**2**). Tracked vehicles fared better 'off road' than wheeled transport, but they were too few or too specialized to be able to carry the volume of supplies needed at the front (**3**). Most transport was thus forced to stick to the few identifiable routes that criss-crossed the desert floor. This made them ideal targets for marauding enemy aircraft. Both sides experienced setbacks in trying to get supplies forward, for the wide open spaces of the desert allowed ground attack aircraft to roam over great distances to seek out and destroy isolated groups of vehicles travelling in convoys. Neither side was able to provide continuous air cover for these columns so each of them had to trust to luck to evade attack by enemy aircraft. By 1942 the performance of the Hurricane fighter was beginning to lag behind that of its more modern German counterparts. It was still in service in the Middle East theatre as the RAF's principal fighter in the desert, but it had by then taken on a number of new roles. The Hurricane had evolved into a versatile fighter capable of undertaking many specialist tasks. Some marks of the Hurricane had their wings strengthened to allow two 110kg bombs to be carried. Other later versions were armed with eight rocket projectiles. One of its most successful deployments in the desert was as a ground attack fighter-bomber. The Hurricane MKIIC shown here was equipped with four 20mm Hispano-Suiza cannons (**4**). The French-designed weapon was able to fire a much heavier weight of projectile than the eight .303in. machine guns that the Hurricane was previously armed with. The larger ammunition, discharged at a rate of ten rounds per second, was better suited against larger targets and was capable of doing great damage during strafing runs against German supply columns. The aircraft shown here was from RAF 274 Squadron. The unit had been in North Africa since December 1940 and had spent its time carrying out fighter operations in the Western Desert along with short periods of defensive duty back in Egypt.

discovered that the whole of his southern flank had collapsed, with the exception of the French in Bir Hacheim who were still in command of their outpost after having beaten off an attack by 50 Italian tanks. Norrie knew that he now had only 1st Armoured Division immediately available with which to counter Rommel's offensive. He ordered Maj. Gen. Lumsden to be ready to move his 1st Armoured Division southwards and advance to battle. First to press forward was 22nd Armoured Brigade, which was then located about 19km north of the scene of 4th Armoured Brigade's encounter with 15.Panzer Division. The 2nd Armoured Brigade was much farther north between Knightsbridge and El Adem when it received Lumsden's order for action. As a precaution, Norrie also moved his corps HQ to the north away from the advancing 90.leichte Division, not wanting to suffer the same fate as Messervy and his headquarters.

Water was precious in the desert and every drop that could be saved was put to good use. Here a soldier is recycling some dirty water using a primitive filter. Unclean water was poured into the top of the empty cans and then descended through layers of sand and small stones to emerge at the bottom, void of much of its earlier contamination. (IWM, E 12283)

The 22nd Armoured Brigade had not gone far before the spearhead of Rommel's advance crashed into it. The two Panzer divisions of the Afrika Korps dealt a devastating blow to the British tanks, and, in just a half an hour of battle, 30 of them had been destroyed. It was soon clear that the enemy were too powerful for this single brigade to resist. Lumsden sent orders to Brigadier Carr for his formation to fall back on Knightsbridge and to regroup. Lumsden ordered Carr to be ready to launch a second blow southwards in concert with a strike from the east by 2nd Armoured Brigade against the German right flank. This counterblow was to have the benefit of the whole of the divisional artillery to support it. The attack was eventually launched in the late afternoon just as the two Panzer divisions were approaching Acroma and Commonwealth Keep. The Panzers were arrayed across the desert slowly grinding their way northwards. They made an impressive sight that was later described by one participant from 44th RTR, as 'a black mass of tanks beginning in the region of Knightsbridge and stretching south as far as the eye could see'. Undeterred by this formidable array of might, the British armour pressed on with some success, for when the two brigades struck Nehring's corps it caused the German Panzers to waver and stop. Then the slower but heavily armoured Matildas of Brigadier O'Carroll's 1st Army Tank Brigade coming in from the west hit the enemy tanks.

The subsequent battle was chaotic and fierce, with many close-quarter actions and tank-versus-tank duels taking place amongst the smoke and haze of the battlefield. One British tank battalion missed the tail of the German armour altogether and slammed into the rear echelons and soft-skinned transport. The tanks did great damage to Rommel's supply line, shooting up every vehicle they came across. The strike also had the good fortune to get between Rommel himself and his armoured columns, cutting off the army commander from the rest of his force for a period of time.

The Afrika Korps had been brought to a halt across the Trig Capuzzo five kilometres north of Knightsbridge and still ten kilometres south of Acroma. It appeared that Rommel's plan was beginning to go awry. The 15.Panzer Division was almost out of fuel and ammunition and its rear echelons were

Some mobility was given to the British 2-pdr anti-tank gun by mounting it on the back of a truck. In the background a PzKpfw III is still smouldering after being knocked out during one of the running tank battles at Gazala. (IWM, E 12792)

being harassed by scattered British forces in the south. The 90.leichte Division was near El Adem but was being contained in its advance by the remnants of 4th Armoured Brigade and the defenders of the El Adem position, the 9th Indian Brigade. The British supply dump at Belhamed seemed to be in no immediate danger. The 132ª Divisione Corazzata 'Ariete' was having no success at removing the French at Bir Hacheim and had advanced northwards on the left flank of Rommel's armoured force only to run into the British 1st Tank Brigade and suffer some loss. The 101ª Divisione Motorizzate 'Trieste' seemed to have disappeared altogether, for no one had heard from the formation since it advanced into the minefields north of Bir Hacheim. Crüwell's attack on the north of the British Gazala Line was bogged down in the minefields and frustrated by a lack of effort on the part of the Italians.

That evening Rommel was counting his losses. It was true that he had dealt a heavy blow to Eighth Army, but at a great cost to his own tank force. The British still had uncommitted armour, including the still to be used army reserve 1st Armoured Brigade and the 32nd Army Tank Brigade in the rear of the Gazala Line, and were at that moment regrouping the tanks scattered by his advance. He had not smashed their armour nor broken their ability to reorganize. In fact, when he looked at his situation on a map it looked precarious. His mobile forces were virtually surrounded: to the west were the South African, British and Free French formations holding an intact Gazala Line; ahead of him were 1st Army Tank Brigade and the two still active brigades of 1st Armoured Division and to the east was the armour and motorized infantry of the 7th Armoured Division. Of further concern were his vulnerable supply lines trailing across the desert in a wide loop around Bir Hacheim subject to harassing attacks by isolated British units and aircraft. That night the Panzerarmee commander confided in his journal: 'Our plan to overrun the British forces behind the Gazala Line had misfired. The opposition was much stronger that expected'.

In the British camp that evening there was some reason for satisfaction. Except for the 3rd Indian Motor Brigade, which had virtually been wiped out as a coherent force, the other brigades had merely been scattered. Of course there had been a high percentage of tank losses, but the numbers of British tanks still outnumbered enemy Panzers by a considerable margin.

Moreover, Rommel's main strike force now seemed to be corralled in an area bounded by Eighth Army's formations. The next few days would prove who was master of the battlefield.

The 28th of May proved to be a day of repositioning and minor encounters. Rommel was still on the offensive, but only with his 21.Panzer Division as the 15.Panzer Division was virtually immobilized that day by shortages of ammunition and fuel. Rommel decided to persevere with his northwards thrust with all available forces. He called the 90.leichte Division back from El Adem and brought the 132ª Divisione Corazzata 'Ariete' up to join him at Bir el Harmat. Both of these formations had to run the gauntlet of British armoured attacks and were unable to rejoin the main force until later that evening.

Rommel ordered Bismarck's 21.Panzer Division to drive for the coast but it only succeeded in reaching Point 209 13km west of Acroma, still eight kilometres short of the sea. The 1st Armoured Division harassed it along the route and, although a few piecemeal attacks were made, the British were not strong enough to completely halt the Panzers. Bismarck's artillery did, however, manage for a while to interdict Allied traffic along the Via Balbia. During its advance, the 21.Panzer Division passed a few kilometres behind Eluet et Tamar and the positions of the uncommitted 32nd Army Tank Brigade, but the British formation did not sally out of its positions to attack, for it had been ordered to stay put and protect the rear of the 1st South African Division holding the Gazala Line. This division was at that moment under attack from the west by Gruppe Crüwell, which was pressing the whole of the northern Gazala Line.

This move northwards was not the bold push Rommel had intended, for 15.Panzer, 90.leichte and the 'Ariete' divisions were all unable to participate because of either supply shortages or British interference. Rommel decided to call back 21.Panzer Division from its exposed position on the escarpment overlooking the Via Balbia to join the main force astride the Trig Capuzzo. Things had not gone smoothly for Rommel that day on a personal front, for while he was absent from his advance HQ at Bir el Harmat visiting Vaerst's division, his command post was overrun by British armour and scattered in the desert. It became clear to Rommel that night that his bid for a quick victory had failed. His position though not critical was certainly insecure.

Later that day, however, Rommel was to receive a small boost to his fortunes. The elusive 101ª Divisione Motorizzate 'Trieste' had been plugging away at the undefended minefield north of Bir Hacheim and had made a breach wide enough to pass a small column through. Its troops were now moving northwards to join Rommel near Bir el Harmat. In doing so the Italians had begun to open up a new shorter supply route that would pass to the left of the Free French position and would therefore be unmolested by British mobile forces. It would nonetheless be some time before the whole route could be made available for the movement of large quantities of supplies. Things got even better for the Germans when the 27ª Divisione 'Brescia' made another breach through the minefields farther to the north, above the box of 150th Brigade, 50th Division.

On 29 May, the fourth day of the battle, the question of supplies still dogged Rommel. Little fuel or ammunition had been supplied to 15.Panzer Division so Rommel took it upon himself to find a means of getting these resources forwards. Early that morning the army commander motored south to find the trucks and lorries of his rear echelons and escort them forwards along a new route that had been recently reconnoitred. It was a dangerous

French colonial troops dig a pit for an old 75mm gun as part of the Free French brigade's defences at Bir Hacheim prior to the start of Rommel's offensive. (IWM, E8009)

move, for the area through which the columns had to motor was alive with British tanks, armoured cars and mobile infantry. Most of the time Rommel found himself under fire and in some personal danger, but his presence at the head of the supply train gave impetus to the replenishment and he soon had the columns up to 15.Panzer Division. By mid-morning the division was ready to resume the offensive.

Moves such as this by Rommel drove his staff to despair. He often spent long periods absent from his headquarters swanning around the desert urging and cajoling his men forwards, leaving those at his command post ignorant of what was happening and unable to communicate with him. However, on this particular day his intervention had at last got his mobile forces regrouped and re-supplied and ready for concerted action. The Afrika Korps, 90.leichte and 'Ariete' divisions were once again together, grouped between the Trig Capuzzo and Trig el Abd to the west of Knightsbridge.

Rommel now decided to go on the defensive in an attempt to recover his balance. He no longer intended to drive northwards to the sea so he called off the proposed seaborne landings by Gruppe Hecker. He proposed to concentrate his mobile force westwards of his present positions and focus his attention on keeping the British armour at bay with a screen of anti-tank guns and artillery facing eastwards. His knew his intended position would be a little exposed, for he would have the British minefields of the Gazala Line to his rear and the tanks of Eighth Army in front, but he did have the corridors through the minefields that the 'Trieste' and 'Brescia' divisions had forged through which he would re-supply his mobile force. His reading of the battlefield suggested that this position would deter the British from attacking westwards from the Gazala Line against the Italians whilst he formed a position from which he could launch a fresh strike eastwards against the heart of Ritchie's army. He was convinced that he had the measure of the situation, confiding in his journal that he foresaw that the British mechanized brigades would continue to 'run their heads against our well-organized defence line and wear themselves down in the process'.

In this he was right, for later that day before Rommel had had a chance to complete his consolidation and was still off balance, Norrie attempted to concentrate all his armour in an attack to try to corner the Germans against the rear of 50th Division's positions in the Gazala Line. Unfortunately, what should have been a show of force degenerated into a disjointed effort that was slow to start and anything but a combined strike. The 15.Panzer Division disrupted the attack from the north by 2nd Armoured Brigade around Knightsbridge, and the 22nd Armoured Brigade's advance in the centre against the 132ª Divisione Corazzata 'Ariete' was disorganized and dispersed by a sandstorm. Nonetheless when these two armoured brigades did get to grips with the enemy, the combat that ensued was both bloody and exhausting. The 4th Armoured Brigade, originally in reserve near El Adem but now sent to reinforce the assault, was also confused by the sandstorm. It arrived too late and was finally turned back after a determined struggle by the anti-tank guns and artillery of the 90.leichte Division.

Eighth Army did have one notable success that day, for they captured one of Rommel's most able generals, Gen.Lt. Crüwell. He had been over-flying the battlefield in a light aircraft in an attempt to pinpoint the extent of 50th Division's positions and was shot down. He was picked up by some British armoured cars and taken into captivity. This should have been a harsh blow for Panzerarmee Afrika, but by good fortune Generalfeldmarschall Kesselring was actually at Crüwell's HQ when news came in of the commanding general's plight. The field marshal immediately stepped in and took command of the situation and remained in control until a suitable replacement arrived to take over this northern group of Rommel's army.

In the extreme north of Ritchie's front, 7th RTR together with a battery of mobile artillery was sent to attack the head of the 21.Panzer Division on Point 209 which was seen to be withdrawing. It had been promised simultaneous support from another column attacking from the east, but this did not materialize. The 7th RTR gallantly ploughed into the Panzers but was turned back with serious loss at the day's end.

REME mechanics working on broken-down or damaged Crusader tanks in a wide-open expanse of the desert. Eighth Army came in for much criticism about the number of damaged tanks that were not recovered from the battlefield and put back into service, but left for the enemy to capture or destroy. The Germans had a very efficient recovery service that removed damaged tanks for repair even while the battle was still raging. (IWM, E13088)

Rommel continued the consolidation of his mobile forces by withdrawing slowly back towards the gaps in the minefields. The move would shorten his front and move his force closer to its new supply routes. He was convinced that once settled in his chosen defensive position he would be even more difficult to dislodge.

During the early hours of the next morning, 30 June, the Afrika Korps continued its westwards withdrawal defended by able rearguards to keep the British at bay. At around 0200hrs it met an acute problem. Near Sidi Muftah it bumped into the British troops manning the box created by 150th Brigade of the 50th Division, reinforced by 30 infantry tanks from 1st Army Tank Brigade. The position dominated the two minefield gaps opened by the Italians and totally disrupted Rommel's plans. He knew it would have to be eliminated and quickly.

The first attack by 15.Panzer Division was halted on the edge of the minefield surrounding the box and then turned back by a screen of British anti-tank guns. While a second assault was being prepared things went from bad to worse for Rommel. At 1100hrs news came in that the British 1st Tank Brigade was attacking 90.leichte Division at Bir Harmat, the 2nd Armoured Brigade was advancing along Trig Capuzzo, 201st Guards Brigade was making a sortie out of the Knightsbridge position to join in the attack and the 21.Panzer Division was being hard pressed by a very heavy bombardment by the guns of the Gazala Line. To make matters worse, the RAF in the shape of the Desert Air Force was up in strength attacking every German column its aircraft could find.

Thus in a short space of time, it seemed that the advantage had swung back in favour of Eighth Army. Victory was within Ritchie's grasp if all these attacks were pressed home together. It seemed that the British commander had Rommel's forces constricted within a relatively small area, bounded by Trig Bir Hacheim, Trig Capuzzo and Trig el Abd, with their backs against the British minefields. The area eventually acquired the nickname of the 'Cauldron'. The 150th Brigade's box dominated the Italian minefield gaps with its artillery, forcing German re-supply to be confined to the night. Rommel's plan to hold the British in the east while consolidating in the west would be impossible as long as the 150th Brigade position held out in his rear.

For a while it seemed so promising for the British, but the ever-confident Rommel was certain of his forces and completely unfazed by the situation. He still thought that he could out-general the British commanders. On the other hand, if things turned really bad for him, he had an escape route to the west through the minefield gaps. Leaving the artillery and anti-tank screen to deal with Eighth Army's attacks, he turned his attention westwards to the problem of 150th Brigade and the Sidi Muftah Box. His confidence was not misplaced for the attacks by the 2nd and 22nd armoured brigades were crushed by his guns and turned back once again with heavy losses, as was that of the 201st Guards Brigade. The British were still not concentrating their armour to an effective degree to enable them to apply the killer blow. During the night supply trucks got through the gaps to the Afrika Korps and both Panzer divisions were refuelled and re-supplied ready once again for concentrated action the next morning. Events had once again swung back in Rommel's favour.

PHASE TWO: THE CAULDRON

The commander of 150th Brigade, Brig. Haydon, had been expecting the German attack for a few days, ever since Rommel's forces had arrived in his rear to the south of Knightsbridge. The gaps above and below his positions effectively meant that his brigade was cut off from the rest of 50th Division and from Eighth Army. Haydon was also hampered in dealing with the Italian gaps by supply difficulties, which had reduced his guns to a ration of

An infantry position of the type seen in the Gazala Line. The breech mechanism of the soldier's .303in. Lee Enfield rifle is wrapped in sacking to prevent sand entering the vital working parts. (IWM, E14751)

just 25 rounds per gun per day. He should have been able to interdict passage through these gaps with his artillery, but he had to conserve shells for the attack from the east that he knew was bound to come. There was no help on hand from the remainder of 50th Division, for the corps commander, Lt. Gen. Gott, had ordered the division's commander, Maj. Gen. Ramsden, not to move out of his positions in the Gazala Line.

Brigadier Haydon knew that the gravest danger was to the rear of his area. It was here that Rommel would strike, so he withdrew a battalion from the south of his positions where it was harassing the 101ᵃ Divisione Motorizzate 'Trieste' and set its men to work digging new trenches and gun pits on the eastern side. Into these new positions the brigadier moved the bulk of his one regiment of 25-pdr guns, the 72nd Field Regiment RA, and a battery of the new 6-pdr anti-tank weapons. Behind these positions was the contingent of tanks from 1st Army Tank Brigade, the 30 Matildas of 44th RTR.

Everyone in the brigade, and indeed elsewhere, knew that this single infantry formation could not hold out for long against armoured opposition, especially when that opposition was the Afrika Korps and its main defensive minefield was to its rear rather than to its front. Rommel had to be engaged in his flanks and rear in order to dilute the strength he could commit against 150th Brigade. At XXX Corps and Eighth Army HQs there was still a good deal of optimism that Rommel had been cornered and could be reduced by shellfire and swept aside by armour. Major-General Lumsden sent an encouraging message to Haydon saying that Eighth Army 'had Rommel boiled'. If an all-round series of continuous and concentrated attacks could be put in then 150th Brigade could be relieved and the battle won.

On 30 May Rommel continued with his attacks against Haydon's isolated brigade box. These were preceded by German engineers moving forwards under covering fire to lift the few mines that had been sown on the eastern side of the position. Motorized infantry then moved forwards and began to penetrate the British position only to be turned back by British infantry supported by the Matildas. Ground was won and lost by successive attacks and counterattacks, and by the end of the day very little new ground had been gained or lost.

Rommel eliminates 150th Brigade's defensive box

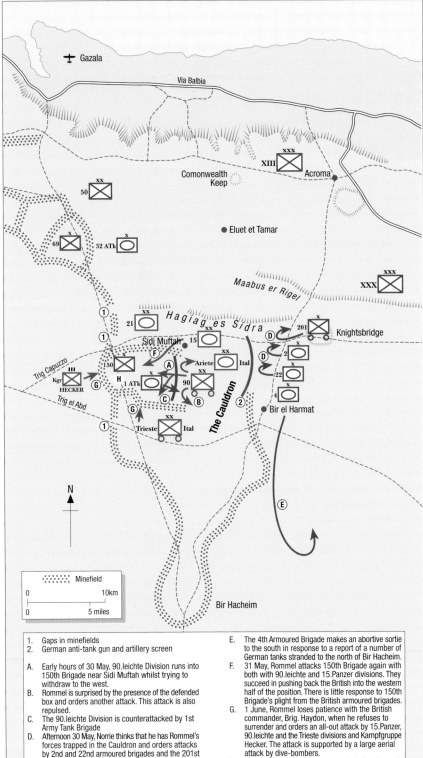

1. Gaps in minefields
2. German anti-tank gun and artillery screen

A. Early hours of 30 May, 90.leichte Division runs into 150th Brigade near Sidi Muftah whilst trying to withdraw to the west.
B. Rommel is surprised by the presence of the defended box and orders another attack. This attack is also repulsed.
C. The 90.leichte Division is counterattacked by 1st Army Tank Brigade
D. Afternoon 30 May, Norrie thinks that he has Rommel's forces trapped in the Cauldron and orders attacks by 2nd and 22nd armoured brigades and the 201st Guards Brigade from the Knightsbridge Box. The enemy anti-tank and artillery screen turns all of these back with great loss.

E. The 4th Armoured Brigade makes an abortive sortie to the south in response to a report of a number of German tanks stranded to the north of Bir Hacheim.
F. 31 May, Rommel attacks 150th Brigade again with both with 90.leichte and 15.Panzer divisions. They succeed in pushing back the British into the western half of the position. There is little response to 150th Brigade's plight from the British armoured brigades.
G. 1 June, Rommel loses patience with the British commander, Brig. Haydon, when he refuses to surrender and orders an all-out attack by 15.Panzer, 90.leichte and the Trieste divisions and Kampfgruppe Hecker. The attack is supported by a large aerial attack by dive-bombers.
H. Late afternoon 1 June, the overwhelming force of the Axis attack eliminates all resistance inside the box and the survivors of 150th Brigade surrender.

A Royal Artillery warrant officer sizes up a captured German 2.8cm Pz. B41 tapered bore 2.8/2.0 anti-tank gun. (IWM, E9090)

Ritchie sent a message to Haydon congratulating him on keeping the enemy at bay: 'Well done!' he signalled. As for positive action to aid the beleaguered brigade, Lumsden organized two diversionary armoured attacks during the daylight hours each of battalion strength, neither of which gave Rommel much cause for concern for they were beaten back by a screen of 90 anti-tank guns along a front much shortened by the Afrika Korps' withdrawal the previous day. The remainder of XXX Corps' armour did very little else that day, although 4th Armoured Brigade made a sortie southwards in search of a reported 30 Panzers and a repair workshop near Bir Hacheim, but found nothing.

The losses to Lumsden's armour led him to complain to Norrie that the only real way to tackle Rommel's force was to have the infantry attack and clear the German anti-tank screens, then for the engineers to lift the defensive minefields to allow the armour to go through. Both Norrie and Ritchie agreed that this was the best course of action and an attack was ordered for the following night, 31 May, with 50th Division's 69th Brigade attacking from the north and one of Eighth Army's reserve formations, 10th Indian Brigade, attacking from the east. In the meantime, 150th Brigade was to hold off the Afrika Korps on its own as best it could, although later that evening a column of one company of infantry, two troops of anti-tank guns and a battery of artillery, set out from Knightsbridge along the Trig Capuzzo to harass the Afrika Korps. They ran into the guns of the 21.Panzer Division, lost five 25-pdrs, seven valuable 6-pdr anti-tank guns and 157 men, and then returned to Knightsbridge. The column achieved nothing save for perhaps the sound of battle giving some comfort to the besieged men of 150th Brigade that at least something was being done to help them.

The next day, 31 May, Rommel issued a formal request for Brig. Haydon to surrender his brigade. The request was rejected without comment by the brigadier. This signalled an intensive artillery bombardment behind which the infantry of the 90.leichte Division crept forwards to the edge of the box. Both sides now became embroiled in close quarter and small arms action. After several hours the Germans withdrew having gained little but having taken a large number of casualties. An hour later the attack was resumed, this time the infantry were backed by tanks. The shock of the assault allowed the British line to be penetrated, but each time a break was opened up it was contained by the determined efforts of the defenders. As the day wore on the fighting became more and more intense until both sides became exhausted and drew back in the failing light of the end of the day.

The area of the box had shrunk to half its size as each successive line of defence had been overwhelmed. Trench systems had been overcome, guns captured or destroyed and isolated resistance posts eliminated. Those weapons that remained intact were very low on ammunition. The time bought by this heroic defence was ill used by the rest of Eighth Army. The infantry attack planned for that night to break into the Cauldron had been postponed by 24 hours – the corps commanders felt that sufficient time had not been available to organize the attack. Ritchie did not send a message to Haydon and his isolated brigade that evening, nor were any diversionary attacks sent in to help them. The 150th Brigade was on its own, left to contain the strength of the four Axis divisions in the Cauldron with whatever means it could.

That night Rommel's forces were re-supplied along the two tracks through the Gazala Line. The next day, 1 June, the army commander decided to put a stop to the stubbornness of Brig. Haydon and his brigade. He ordered an assault of massive proportions to eliminate what had become a tiresome diversion to his plans. The heaviest possible aerial attack would be mounted on the Sidi Muftah Box by the Luftwaffe to be followed by a massed tank and infantry assault on its defences. He intended that brute force would overwhelm the British in a blatant show of might.

As expected, this demonstration of the Axis power won through that day. The defensive box was crushed mercilessly, but only after a long and bitter struggle. An enemy report written after the battle talked of the stubborn resistance and hand-to-hand fighting that was met at each bunker and defence position in turn, with the British suffering extraordinarily heavy, bloody losses. At one point during the height of the action, Rommel himself took personal command of one of the leading platoons. As a later historian pointed out, this was possibly the first time a unit of such small size was commanded in action by so high-ranking an officer. Soon every British position had been

A cheerful group of motorized infantry from 15.Panzer Division are thankful to be once again out of the line after a stiff encounter with Eighth Army. (IWM, NA1815)

The crew of an Italian anti-tank gun from the 101ª Divisione Motorizzate 'Trieste' watch the bombing of French positions in Bir Hacheim by German dive-bombers early in June 1942. (IWM, MH5850)

surrounded or destroyed; ammunition stocks dwindled to nothing; the fight was knocked out of the beleaguered defenders. Finally an end was called and the fighting ceased. The 150th Brigade capitulated to the victors and 3,000 British survivors filed into captivity. Rommel rushed forwards to the brigade's headquarters to congratulate Haydon upon the courage and skill of his men, but to his sincere sorrow he found that the brigadier had been killed by shellfire earlier in the day.

Details concerning the loss of 150th Brigade did not reach Ritchie until late that night. In the meantime the army commander continued with his plan for a two-brigade infantry attack on the Cauldron from the north and east, with 150th Brigade attacking simultaneously out of its defensive box towards the east. Ritchie might have believed that this was what was going to happen, but his corps commanders were making other plans. Gott's XIII Corps was not now going to use 50th Division's 69th Brigade, but decided that the 151st Brigade, positioned to the north of 69th Brigade, would in fact take over the attack. In the event, the divisional commander felt that only one battalion could be released for the operation. Of XXX Corps' contribution, 10th Indian Brigade took so long advancing down from Tobruk to the start line, despite having two days to organize the move, that Maj. Gen. Messervy, under whose command the 10th Indian Brigade had been placed, called off the attack and informed Norrie only after he had made the decision. So there it was, Ritchie's great plan to drive into the Cauldron and relieve 150th Brigade had shrunk to just a single battalion attack which, not surprisingly, failed to reach even its first objective when it was launched that night.

When news finally did reach Ritchie of the demise of Haydon's brigade, he was saddened by the loss but felt that circumstances were 'still favourable and getting better daily'. He saw the situation as his army surrounding and containing Rommel's forces whilst gradually applying enough pressure to squeeze it to death. General Auchinleck saw things differently; with Auchinleck it was more the case of the enemy having a very strong salient driven into Eighth Army's line. He signalled Ritchie to beware that his army was not in danger of losing the initiative.

With the defeat of 150th Brigade, Rommel now had a clear route to his supply dumps to the west. His actions had manoeuvred his force into a

strong, concentrated position with his mobile group capable of being reinforced and re-supplied unhindered. He knew that the British would attack him again whilst he was static in the Cauldron, but felt assured that his force would be able to absorb the blow when it came and that the tactics Ritchie would employ would be predictable and pedestrian.

In the meantime, there was the irritation of having a French brigade at liberty in the south at Bir Hacheim with the means of harassing his extreme right flank. It would have to be eliminated and on 2 June Rommel sent the 'Trieste' and 90.leichte divisions, together with a few tanks of the 132^a Divisione Corazzata 'Ariete', southwards to deal with the problem. To draw Eighth Army's attention away from the attacks on Bir Hacheim, Rommel sent the 21.Panzer Division on a sortie to the north against Eluet et Tamar. It was a diversion, but nonetheless it induced 4th Armoured Brigade to send 5th RTR to investigate, during which time the British lost 12 tanks. Then things settled down for few days whilst both sides sorted out their armour and planned their next moves.

The Bir Hacheim Box was held by Gén. de brig. Koenig's 1ère Brigade Française Libre (BFL) consisting of six battalions of infantry of which two were from the 13e Demi-Brigade de la Légion Étrangère (DBLE), a battalion of artillery and a company of anti-tank guns. In terms of firepower, at the start of the battle the brigade could deploy 26 field guns – mostly obsolete 75mm guns – 62 anti-tank guns of various sizes and 44 mortars. The Bir Hacheim position was virtually featureless, consisting of a barren expanse of desert into

The headquarters' tanks of one of Eighth Army's armoured brigades on 31 May 1942. The cheerful faces reflect the growing belief that Rommel had become trapped in the Cauldron and was about to be annihilated by Eighth Army. The Grant's high silhouette, which made the cruiser tank visible from a great distance, is clearly illustrated. (IWM, E12637)

which the French had carved out an area of trenches, gun emplacements and defence posts, almost all of which were below ground level.

On 3 June the gathering German and Italian troops and transport around Bir Hacheim gave the Desert Air Force easily identifiable targets for their bombing and strafing raids. Scores of burning lorries and vehicles soon littered the desert floor on the approaches to the besieged garrison and gave great heart to the French defenders. 'Bravo! Merci pour la RAF', signalled Koenig to Air Vice-Marshal Coningham.

The attacks on Bir Hacheim made by the 'Trieste' and 90.leichte divisions made little progress over the next few days for the resistance put up by the Free French surprised everyone. Their positions were skilfully placed and resolutely defended with extended minefields and well-sited anti-tank guns making it extremely costly for the Axis divisions to penetrate the perimeter of the box. Attacks by the Luftwaffe had difficulty pinpointing individual resistance posts so carefully did they blend with the desert floor.

Back in the centre of the battlefield, Auchinleck and Ritchie were deciding what to do next. Auchinleck favoured making a bold thrust out of XIII Corps' defence positions and heading for Bir el Temrad in the Axis rear, 16km to the west of the Gazala Line. Ritchie and his corps commanders were against such a move, claiming that they might not be able to hold Rommel's armour while such a bold advance was made. The same reason was true for another of Auchinleck's suggestions, that of making a wide turning movement round the southern flank. Ritchie decided that the best course of action would be first to crush the enemy's mobile forces contained in the Cauldron. That was exactly what Rommel expected him to do.

Ritchie's attempt at eliminating Rommel's forces in the Cauldron, Operation *Aberdeen*, was timed for the night of 4/5 June and was to be completed in two phases: first, the 10th Indian Brigade of Maj. Gen. Briggs's 5th Indian Division would attack from the east following a heavy artillery barrage and achieve a break-in through Rommel's defensive minefields and anti-tank guns, followed by the 32nd Army Tank Brigade attacking from the north to capture the Sidra Ridge overlooking the Cauldron; second, the main role would switch to Messervy's 7th Armoured Division, with 9th Indian Brigade under command, whose task was to destroy the enemy in the Cauldron itself. The 1st Armoured Division was initially charged with preventing Rommel breaking out to the north or north-east, then, as the battle progressed, the division would be ready to exploit success westwards.

The battle started at 0250hrs on 5 June and the attack by 10th Indian Brigade made good immediate progress to its initial objectives with very few casualties. By daylight the eastern flank of the Cauldron had been penetrated and the situation was ready for the armour and the second infantry brigade (9th Indian Brigade) to go through. The 22nd Armoured Brigade – temporarily moved into 7th Armoured Division to replace the tired and battered 4th Armoured Brigade – advanced with 156 Grant, Stuart and Crusader tanks to a depth of three kilometres before the Germans struck back. It was with great shock that the tanks found Rommel's main defence line had been moved back and the initial British artillery bombardment had fallen on barren ground. Now enemy fire hit the advancing tanks with devastating effect, slewing the majority of the armour out of line and doing great destruction. The whole brigade veered to the north trying to escape the wrath of the German tank, anti-tank and artillery fire. Unable to manoeuvre its way clear, 22nd Armoured Brigade escaped from the mêlée by then turning north-east to seek refuge behind the Knightsbridge position. Messervy had been initially instructed that his armoured advance was to assist the 9th Indian Brigade at the outset, but his main task was to destroy the enemy's tanks. His orders specifically stated that 'in case of armoured action infantry are self-protecting and were not to hamper the movement of 22nd Armoured Brigade'. In view of these orders, 22nd Armoured Brigade quit the battlefield after its contact with the enemy armour and left the infantry of the 9th and 10th Indian brigades to fend for themselves.

In the north, 32nd Army Tank Brigade's dawn attack on the Sidra Ridge failed miserably. It had run into an unexpected enemy minefield and was then hit by the 21.Panzer Division's anti-tank screen. Intense and accurate shellfire tore into the slow-moving infantry tanks and by the time the attack was called off the brigade had lost 50 of the 70 tanks with which it had begun the battle.

At their headquarters, the two divisional generals were dismayed by the turn of events. Each now became preoccupied with his own problems. Both commanders were anxious to hold on, but nobody was available to decide what had to be done to regain the initiative. Apart from the army commander himself, there was nobody in sole command to run the battle that was taking place on two separate fronts. The 2nd Armoured Brigade, reinforced with a battalion of motorized infantry and a regiment of field artillery, was sent to a position south of Knightsbridge and placed under Maj. Gen. Messervy's command, but ended up receiving a number of orders from 7th Armoured Division, each of which cancelled out the previous.

By mid-afternoon Rommel sensed that the British had shot their bolt and ordered the Afrika Korps and the 132[a] Divisione Corazzata 'Ariete' to take advantage of the situation and to strike east and north-east. Their advance sent Ritchie's forces reeling in confusion. The tactical headquarters of both the 5th Indian and the 7th Armoured divisions were forced to scatter from the path of the onrushing enemy armour, as were those of various other brigades and battalions. Once again, Maj. Gen. Messervy found himself out of touch

Operation *Aberdeen*: Ritchie's attempt to crush Rommel's forces in the Cauldron on 5 June

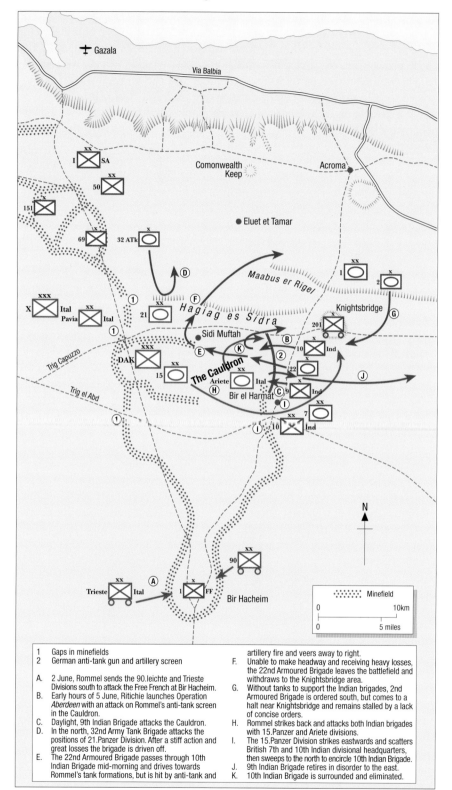

1   Gaps in minefields
2   German anti-tank gun and artillery screen

A. 2 June, Rommel sends the 90.leichte and Trieste Divisions south to attack the Free French at Bir Hacheim.
B. Early hours of 5 June, Ritichie launches Operation *Aberdeen* with an attack on Rommel's anti-tank screen in the Cauldron.
C. Daylight, 9th Indian Brigade attacks the Cauldron.
D. In the north, 32nd Army Tank Brigade attacks the positions of 21.Panzer Division. After a stiff action and great losses the brigade is driven off.
E. The 22nd Armoured Brigade passes through 10th Indian Brigade mid-morning and drives towards Rommel's tank formations, but is hit by anti-tank and artillery fire and veers away to right.
F. Unable to make headway and receiving heavy losses, the 22nd Armoured Brigade leaves the battlefield and withdraws to the Knightsbridge area.
G. Without tanks to support the Indian brigades, 2nd Armoured Brigade is ordered south, but comes to a halt near Knightsbridge and remains stalled by a lack of concise orders.
H. Rommel strikes back and attacks both Indian brigades with 15.Panzer and Ariete divisions.
I. The 15.Panzer Division strikes eastwards and scatters British 7th and 10th Indian divisional headquarters, then sweeps to the north to encircle 10th Indian Brigade.
J. 9th Indian Brigade retires in disorder to the east.
K. 10th Indian Brigade is surrounded and eliminated.

with his command, fleeing into the desert. A sweeping movement by 15.Panzer Division scattered the whole of the 9th Indian Brigade and completely enveloped the 10th Indian Brigade. Whilst things did not degenerate into a state of actual panic, the British Official History later explained that it was close: 'Communication and control broke down completely'. Rommel was content for his mobile forces just to rout the opposition and chase it back into its prepared positions of Knightsbridge and El Adem. He had seen off another attempt to break into his lines, but was not quite ready to renew his own offensive.

Losses that day had been considerable for Eighth Army; the 22nd Armoured Brigade alone had lost 60 of its 156 tanks during Operation *Aberdeen*. All three armoured brigades, the 2nd, 4th and 22nd, were now placed under the command of 7th Armoured Division with the intention of rescuing the 10th Indian Brigade, but as the historian of the Royal Tank Regiment put it: 'The intention evaporated in delays, misunderstood orders, counter-orders and disorder.'

With the British armour chased away, Rommel's force now turned to deal with the British and Indian infantry and artillery left inside the Cauldron. There was no help for the doomed units now totally surrounded by the enemy. On 6 June, after dramatic and bloody resistance, the 4th/10th Baluch Regiment, the 2nd/4th Gurkha Rifles, the 3rd/9th Jat Regiment, the 50th Reconnaissance Regiment, the 4th, 28th and 157th field regiments Royal Artillery and the 107th Regiment Royal Horse Artillery were overrun and eliminated. 'The gunners fought their guns to the last and died where they stood' noted the divisional history. All of 5th Indian Division's artillery had been captured along with 4,000 of its troops.

Rommel was scathing in his criticism of Eighth Army. He could not understand why its commander did not throw all the strength he could muster into the battle. He had after all three divisions sitting still doing very little – the 1st South African, the 50th and the 1st Armoured Division. 'What is the use of having overall superiority', he wrote in his journal, 'if one allows each formation to be smashed piecemeal by an enemy who is able to concentrate superior forces on every occasion at the decisive point?'

One of Eighth Army's Grant tanks passes a vastly inferior PzKpfw II, which has been knocked out in action the previous day. The picture was taken on 6 June 1942, the day after Ritchie's disastrous attack on the Cauldron, Operation *Aberdeen*. (IWM, 12919)

After soundly defeating the British, Rommel could now concentrate on eliminating the French outpost at Bir Hacheim. The forces originally designated with overthrowing the most southerly of Eighth Army's boxes, the 'Trieste' and 90.leichte divisions, had found the task to be more difficult than anticipated. Général de brigade Koenig's men were fighting with a tenacity that was beginning to capture the world's attention and restore some pride to French arms.

On the evening of 6 June, Rommel sent a Panzer battlegroup from 15.Panzer Division south to reinforce the assault on Bir Hacheim. The remainder of his armour stayed close to Knightsbridge – sarcastically christened 'Servantsbridge' by the Germans – in order to keep the British tanks pinned down. Ritchie could not now move his tank force without leaving the way open for Rommel to make a move against either Tobruk or the great supply dump at Belhamed. Over the next few days Eighth Army was content to prick away at the enemy with small strokes, smash and grab raids against the flanks of Rommel's force, seizing prisoners and knocking out exposed tanks and transport.

Meanwhile, at Bir Hacheim, a renewed and reinforced assault was made by Axis forces to capture the defensive box on 7 June. The previous day Ritchie had considered giving up the French position now that the enemy had established a more direct supply route through the Gazala Line minefields into the area of the Cauldron, but Auchinleck advised against relinquishing this outpost as it still guarded a possible route round Rommel's forces if and when a new offensive to the west was launched. It was rather wishful thinking on the Commander-in-Chief's part to expect that the French garrison could hold out indefinitely while some possible attack was being initiated at some indeterminate time in the future, when Panzer-led assaults were taking place daily against what were essentially infantry positions.

Despite the whole area coming under concerted air assault by the Luftwaffe, French anti-tank guns and artillery once again repulsed the Axis attack on 7 June. Rommel now insisted that the position should be taken the next day and sent another *Kampfgruppe* from 15.Panzer Division and the whole of Gruppe Hecker southwards to help in the assault. On 8 June the

Luftwaffe stepped up its raids on Bir Hacheim, sending 45 bombers and 54 single-engine fighters against its targets. This was followed by infantry and tank attacks, each of which was beaten back by the French. Général de brigade Koenig signalled that his men were exhausted by the continual fighting and needed a full-scale operation to relieve them, along with more air support.

The first request was unable to be accommodated; it was too short notice for Norrie's corps to be able to respond, although why some relief for the siege had not already been organized days before is a mystery. The 7th Motor Brigade and the 29th Indian Brigade were in the area harassing enemy communications, but their role did not apparently include going to the aid of comrades who were fighting for their lives. Air support, however, was given and the Desert Air Force flew 478 sorties that day, the highest total for one day thus far in the desert war. One German and three Italian aircraft were destroyed for the loss of eight of the RAF's aircraft.

To Rommel's annoyance, Bir Hacheim did not fall on 8 June and so the attacks resumed on the 9th. Air attacks and heavy shelling continued to blast the barren desert strongpoint all day. Enemy tanks and infantry assaulted twice more, each time achieving a breach in the defences and each time being evicted from within the perimeter. Lieutenant-General Norrie's XXX Corps tried to respond to a plea for help by sending elements of the 4th Armoured, 7th Motor and 29th Indian brigades against the flanks of the enemy, but their attacks were not strong enough to cause the Axis forces any problems, although the 90.leichte Division had to turn and defend itself against one of the armoured columns.

Inside the Bir Hacheim Box things gradually became critical. The perimeter of the defensive area was shrinking rapidly as more and more of the French trenches and gun pits were overrun after each new assault. Koenig's

THE DEFENCE OF BIR HACHEIM, 26 MAY TO 11 JUNE 1942 (pp. 60–61)

The remote defensive 'box' at Bir Hacheim was constructed on the former site of a Turkish fort and consisted mainly of interconnecting field fortifications, trenches and gun emplacements (1). It stood astride the crossroads of two Bedouin tracks in the middle of the arid desert; a barren rocky place, windswept and desolate. The battlefield was almost completely flat, marked by a total absence of cover and natural obstacles. In May 1942 it was garrisoned by Gén. de brig. Marie Pierre Koenig's 1ère Brigade Française Libre, consisting of six battalions of infantry of which two, the 2e and 3e bataillons, were from the 13e Demi-Brigade de Légion Étrangère (DBLE), a battalion of artillery and a company of anti-tank guns, in all about 3,700 men. The scene shows legionnaires, assisted by a gun crew from Colonel Laurent-Champrosay's 1ère Regiment d'Artillerie, dealing with an Axis infantry attack supported by Italian M13/40 tanks (2). The gun's crew are French but are equipped with British uniforms, helmets and personal weapons. (3) The gun itself is a rather ancient 75mm weapon (4), one of a number of guns which the 1ère Brigade Française Libre had received from the Vichy French stores in the Levant states of Syria and Lebanon after the fighting there the previous year. The version of the famous 75mm field gun used at Bir Hacheim

had been converted to the MLE 1897/1940 specification and was used mainly in an anti-tank role. Modern pneumatic tyres had been fitted in place of the original wooden wheels and the gun shield cut down to reduce the weapon's silhouette. One of the original guns actually used in the defence of Bir Hacheim is now in the Musée de l'Armée in Paris. Koenig's forces were supplied with British uniforms, equipment and transport (mainly Bren carriers), but were mostly armed with French weapons (5). They kept their standard rifle, the French type MAS36, together with their mortars, Hotchkiss machine guns and anti-aircraft weapons. The backbone of the defence was the two battalions of the Légion Étrangère and it is doubtful that any other military unit had a more nomadic journey during World War II than the 13e DBLE. The legionnaires fought from the frozen fjords of Norway in 1940, throughout the battlefields of North Africa and the Middle East, then in the mountains of Italy in 1943, into France in 1944 and finally across the border into Germany in 1945 towards the end of the war. The unit was raised in January 1940 specifically to aid the Finns in their struggle against invasion by the Soviet Union, but the collapse of Finland in March of that year led to the 13e DBLE moving to Norway in an Anglo-French attempt to deny that country to the Germans.

Jubilant troops of Koenig's Free French brigade celebrate reaching the British lines after their escape from the siege at Bir Hacheim. Out of a garrison of around 3,600 men at the start of the battle, over 2,600 managed to get away from the encirclement. (IWM, E13387)

men had been in action since the start of the battle on 27 May and were now very tired. Each time one of the defensive positions manned by the brave colonial troops from Chad and the Congo was pushed back, parties from the Légion Étrangère would rush forwards to fill the gaps. Morale remained remarkably high, for Koenig's men knew that they were on their own, fighting for the honour of France with the eyes of the world on their heroic struggle. Ammunition and supplies were running out, medical facilities were overstretched and re-supply by those units of 7th Motor Brigade who were able to slip through the Axis ring surrounding the fortress was becoming impossible. With no relief and no new supplies, it was evident to all that the end of the Bir Hacheim Box was near.

The next day, 10 June, Ritchie decided that the garrison should withdraw during the hours of darkness. Plans in fact were already afoot, for Messervy had spoken with Koenig the previous day and advised him that it was time to pull out. Koenig asked for transport to be brought as close as possible so that the wounded might be evacuated, but the move could not be arranged for that night and so was laid on for the following one.

By this time Rommel had had enough. He moved down to Bir Hacheim and took control of what he was expecting to be the final assault. Throughout that day the storming parties of motorized infantry once again worked their way through the minefields, wire defences and shellfire to close with the French. In the afternoon the Luftwaffe made their heaviest bombing raid of all on the shrinking perimeter held by Koenig's men. As daylight faded the guns and mortars began to fire the last of their ammunition and the colonial infantry and legionnaires fended off desperate, almost fanatical, German assaults with hand-to-hand combat. The enemy was closing in for the final push; it was time to go.

French engineers now began to clear a gap through their minefield for an escape route and all transport that was still movable was loaded with the wounded and made ready to move. Two companies were detailed to remain behind to maintain contact with the enemy and to mask the retreat. Then word was finally passed along the lines and outposts for the withdrawal to begin. It was not an easy task, but a disciplined evacuation was conducted, although at times fraught with danger and problems. After a while the enemy realized what was happening and strafed and mortared the area to the west. Parachute flares went up and bathed the desert air in brilliant white light, probing the area to find the route of the retreat. Machine guns rattled and artillery shells whined, but through the mêlée the French slipped away to rendezvous with the lorries of 7th Motor Brigade. By the end of the withdrawal, after a few days had passed and the final stragglers had made their way to safety, it was found that Général de brigade Koenig and 2,700 of his men had reached sanctuary out of the 3,600 troops that had garrisoned Bir Hacheim at the start of the battle. Their long struggle had bought time for Eighth Army and the heroism of their resistance had restored pride to the French nation.

PHASE THREE: THE FAILURE OF THE BRITISH ARMOUR

The time gained by Eighth Army through Rommel's preoccupation with the French defence of the Bir Hacheim Box had been put to little use. XXX Corps contented itself with moving behind the defences of the protected boxes at Knightsbridge and El Adem to await the enemy's next attack. One later historian compared this inactivity to a flock of sheep awaiting their fate at the fangs of marauding wolves. General Auchinleck hoped that Rommel might be induced to attack the strong British positions and exhaust himself. The main problem was that Norrie and his armoured commanders were plagued with doubts about the likelihood of their ever being able to beat Rommel's forces. So many tank attacks had resulted in failure and great losses. It was true that the enemy was also suffering considerable losses to its armoured force, but he had almost always held the initiative. After each action, when the two sides pulled back, it was usually the British who felt the sharp pangs of defeat.

On paper, Ritchie's forces were still greater than Rommel's. Five of the seven infantry brigades that were in the Gazala Line when the enemy offensive began had seen very little of the fighting and Ritchie's strength was still on the increase for two new brigades, the 11th from 4th Indian Division and the 20th from 10th Indian Division, had just arrived in the battle area from Egypt and Iraq. As for tanks, on 11 June the two armoured divisions could muster 185 cruisers, 77 of which were Grants, and the 32nd Army Tank Brigade had 85 serviceable Matilda and Valentine infantry tanks. On the other hand, it was estimated that Rommel had just over 200 tanks, 85 of which were the inferior Italian M13s and Panzer IIs.

However, after so many setbacks the morale of the British armoured brigades was starting to fall. Having to accept so many losses and to absorb so many new faces from other formations was denting unit pride.

The crew of the Crusader tank 'Cynig' wait for the order to move forwards and into battle. The tank could be from the 3rd Royal Tank Regiment of 4th Armoured Brigade, as all of the regiment's tanks began with the letter 'C' – those of 4th RTR began with 'D', 5th RTR with 'E', etc. (IWM, E8076)

Replacement tanks often arrived in such poor condition that they needed maintenance before they went into action. Survivors of so many tank actions were beginning to become fatalistic and sensed ultimate defeat. Tank crews were losing confidence in their commanders. Friction was also growing between the various generals as frustrations and setbacks continued: Maj. Gen. Pienaar and Lt. Gen. Gott were losing respect for each other and the relationship between the two armoured division commanders, Lumsden and Messervy, was at an all-time low. This animosity was detected by junior commanders and affected the smooth running of the respective formations. The interchanging of units between formations complicated the chain of command; each of the armoured brigades had changed divisions at least twice. Ritchie's corps commanders, Norrie and Gott, were forceful in their objections to many of the proposals that the army commander put forwards and Ritchie was not a strong enough personality to stamp his authority on these men. Time and again his corps commanders questioned his orders.

With loss of the southern half of the battlefield, the British defence line was shortened and had swung eastwards. It now ran along the original northern part of the Gazala Line from the sea down to south of Alem Hamza where it was still held by the 1st South African and 50th Divisions. Action along this part of the front had begun with the attacks by Gruppe Crüwell, containing the Italian X and XXI corps, on the first day of the battle, but the fighting never escalated to a point where it gave concern that a breakthrough might be made. From Alem Hamza across to Acroma five new small boxes had been established, each containing a battalion of infantry, a field battery of artillery and a few anti-tank guns. Knightsbridge was still held by the 201st Guards Brigade Group, whilst the 29th Indian Brigade held the El Adem locality. Tobruk remained garrisoned by the 2nd South African Division and there were smaller defended localities at Sidi Rezegh and Belhamed. The armour was grouped between Knightsbridge and El Adem.

At Bir Hacheim Rommel allowed himself a short time to visit and appreciate the defence system that the French had built before he turned his attention back to the business in the north. He called his commanders together and briefed them on the resumption of his advance. He intended that he would continue with the main objectives of Operation *Venezia*, his original plan at the start of the offensive. The 90.leichte Division would once more move along his right flank, pass south of El Adem and make for the British supply centre at Belhamed. The 15.Panzer and the 'Trieste' divisions would take the left flank and strike between El Adem and Knightsbridge directly towards Tobruk, with their first objective being the airfield to the north of El Adem. The 21.Panzer and the 'Ariete' divisions, still in the vicinity of the Cauldron, would protect the main supply routes to the west, hold down the British infantry along their new defence line and threaten the British armour around Knightsbridge.

Rommel had his forces on the move again by the middle of the afternoon of 11 June. The advance by the 90.leichte Division was soon subjected to flank attacks by the 7th Motor Brigade and two columns of Indian troops who were still located in the southern desert, but they were more of a nuisance than full-blown counterattacks. The advance was soon picked up by the RAF and reported to Norrie who immediately set Brig. Richards' 4th Armoured Brigade moving south-east from Knightsbridge. By the evening, the armoured brigade had reached a ridge of high ground at Naduret el Ghesceuasc and remained there for the night. By this time the 15.Panzer Division had come up and they too stopped to rest a few miles to the south-east of the British armoured brigade, just within shelling distance.

During the night Norrie decided that if he reinforced 7th Armoured Division with the tanks of 2nd Armoured Brigade, Messervy would have sufficient strength to sweep down from the high ground and attack the 15.Panzer Division in the flank. Even with this shift of armour, Norrie felt that he would have enough tanks around Knightsbridge in 22nd Armoured and 32nd Army Tank brigades to deal with the other two Axis divisions in the Cauldron area.

The plan, however, did not materialize for Lumsden was loath to hand over one of his brigades to Messervy. In turn, Messervy wished to concentrate his division by moving the 4th Armoured Brigade around the southern flank of 15.Panzer Division to join with his 7th Motor Brigade and fight as a division. To further complicate matters, the commander of 4th Armoured Brigade, Brig. Richards, did not like Messervy's plan and wished to hold the high ground at Ghesceuasc while the commander of 2nd Armoured Brigade, Brig. Briggs, wished to return to 1st Armoured Division. Messervy was furious with the two brigadiers and set off to confer with Norrie. En route to XXX Corps HQ, for the third time in the battle he became out of touch with his division when he was almost caught by an enemy patrol and spent the whole of the day hiding in a disused well in the desert. In the meantime, the commanders of both the 2nd and 4th armoured brigades sat in position and waited for further orders.

During this time 15.Panzer Division turned northwards and moved against the two British armoured brigades. The attack did not really get going and was held at bay by the Grants of the two British formations. Early in the afternoon, Norrie realized that Messervy was out of contact and placed all the armour under Lumsden. He also noticed that Rommel had spread his mobile forces over a large area and felt that the time was right to launch an attack

German troops inspect a captured Crusader tank knocked out during one of the Gazala battles. (IWM, MH5571)

into their flanks. He ordered the 22nd Armoured Brigade forwards from Knightsbridge so that all of his corps' armour was gathered together for the attack. But before this could take place, Rommel had come up to the 15.Panzer Division to join with the Afrika Korps' commander, Gen.Lt. Nehring, and ordered a renewed attack against the British. Together these two generals put some energy back into the Panzer division and set the tanks off again towards XXX Corps' positions. Coordinated with this move was a shift by 21.Panzer Division across from the west to join in the battle.

The British armour in the Ghesceuasc area watched the Panzer attack sweep forwards and up onto the rising ground in front of them. With Rommel and Nehring driving the tanks on, the attack went in with great ferocity. Very soon both sides became engaged in tank-versus-tank action. Then, from almost out of nowhere, the 21.Panzer Division crashed into the right flank of the 4th Armoured Brigade. In a very short while, the brigade had lost 20 tanks and was forced to turn to face the enemy. Now dealing with an enemy on two fronts, the British began to give ground. Matters became more complicated when German anti-tank guns came forwards and began shelling the British armour from the other flank. It seemed to Lumsden's men that they were surrounded. Fortunately, the arrival of the 22nd Armoured Brigade helped stem the German advance and allowed 4th Armoured Brigade to extricate itself from the mêlée and to withdraw in some disorder to the north-east where it finally came to a halt close to Tobruk along the El Adem–Acroma road. Its armour had been reduced to just 15 fully working tanks.

Lumsden now ordered the remaining two brigades to fall back to the east of Knightsbridge. The two German divisions also moved northwards; the 15.Panzer Division to a position between the British armour and El Adem, the 21.Panzer Division to the western side of Knightsbridge. Farther to the east, the 90.leichte Division had advanced past the eastern flank of El Adem into a position between the bulk of Eighth Army and the large supply dump at Belhamed. The action of 12 June had been costly for the British armour; 138 tanks had been lost in one afternoon.

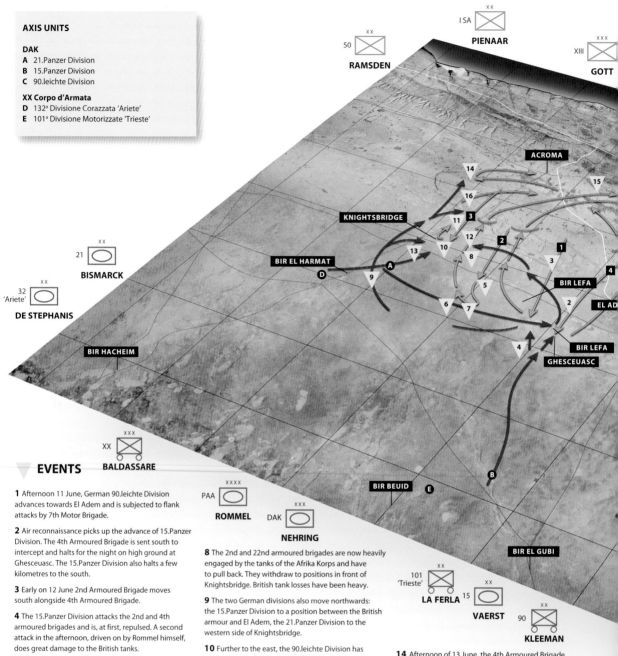

AXIS UNITS

DAK
A 21.Panzer Division
B 15.Panzer Division
C 90.leichte Division

XX Corpo d'Armata
D 132ª Divisione Corazzata 'Ariete'
E 101ª Divisione Motorizzate 'Trieste'

EVENTS

1 Afternoon 11 June, German 90.leichte Division advances towards El Adem and is subjected to flank attacks by 7th Motor Brigade.

2 Air reconnaissance picks up the advance of 15.Panzer Division. The 4th Armoured Brigade is sent south to intercept and halts for the night on high ground at Ghesceuasc. The 15.Panzer Division also halts a few kilometres to the south.

3 Early on 12 June 2nd Armoured Brigade moves south alongside 4th Armoured Brigade.

4 The 15.Panzer Division attacks the 2nd and 4th armoured brigades and is, at first, repulsed. A second attack in the afternoon, driven on by Rommel himself, does great damage to the British tanks.

5 Lieutenant-General Norrie, commander XXX Corps, realizes that Rommel's armour is now stretched out and orders 22nd Armoured Brigade southwards to strike 15.Panzer Division in the flank.

6 Before 22nd Armoured Brigade can intervene, 4th Armoured Brigade is hit in its right flank by 21.Panzer Division which has moved across from the west of Knightsbridge.

7 The arrival of 22nd Armoured Brigade unbalances 21.Panzer Division and allows 4th Armoured Brigade to retire to the area south of Acroma.

8 The 2nd and 22nd armoured brigades are now heavily engaged by the tanks of the Afrika Korps and have to pull back. They withdraw to positions in front of Knightsbridge. British tank losses have been heavy.

9 The two German divisions also move northwards: the 15.Panzer Division to a position between the British armour and El Adem, the 21.Panzer Division to the western side of Knightsbridge.

10 Further to the east, the 90.leichte Division has advanced past the eastern flank of El Adem into a position between the bulk of Eighth Army and the large supply dump at Belhamed.

11 Infantry tanks of 32nd Army Tank Brigade support the 201st Guards (Motor) Brigade in the Knightsbridge Box.

12 13 June, 15.Panzer Division attacks the Knightsbridge Box from the west and pushes both British armoured brigades northwards.

13 21.Panzer, 'Ariete' and the 15.Panzer divisions attack the 201st Guards (Motor) Brigade's positions in the Knightsbridge Box from three sides.

14 Afternoon of 13 June, the 4th Armoured Brigade comes south to block elements of the 21.Panzer Division attempting to advance northwards to the coast.

15 Evening 13 June, the three armoured brigades and the army tank brigade are unable to hold the Afrika Korps and begin to retire eastwards.

16 Now almost surrounded, the 201st Guards (Motor) Brigade is withdrawn from the Knightsbridge Box back to the area east of Tobruk leaving Rommel's forces in complete command of the whole of the southern sector of Eighth Army's battlefield.

THE DECISIVE ARMOURED ACTIONS OF 12 AND 13 JUNE 1942

The British armour is comprehensively defeated by Rommel to the south-east of the Knightsbridge Box.

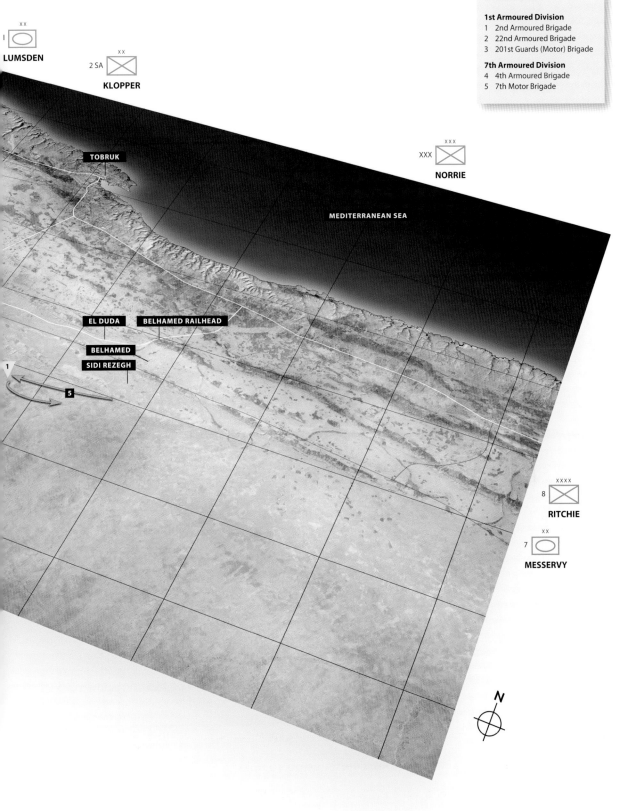

Note: Gridlines are shown at intervals of 10km/6.21 miles

LUMSDEN

2 SA

KLOPPER

TOBRUK

NORRIE

MEDITERRANEAN SEA

EL DUDA   BELHAMED RAILHEAD

BELHAMED

SIDI REZEGH

1

5

8

RITCHIE

7

MESSERVY

N

Lieutenant-General Norrie, Commander British XXX Corps (left), studies a map with his ADC. The fact that the armour of XXX Corps did not perform well during the Gazala battles was not solely a result of the inferiority of its tanks, the performance of Norrie's subordinate commanders were also much to blame. (IWM, E12264)

On 13 June it was clear to Ritchie that Rommel was in a strong position to drive northwards to the coast and cut off the bulk of Gott's XIII Corps. Such a move would isolate both the 1st South African and the 50th divisions. The army commander was now faced with two choices; either he had to stand and fight, or he had to withdraw eastwards, probably right back to the frontier with Egypt. Both options carried great risks. If he stood firm his now-depleted armour would most likely be destroyed leaving the infantry divisions cut off, and if he retreated he would be involved in a running fight that could also end in disaster and Tobruk would be left to the enemy.

Ritchie chose to stand and fight, a decision that was approved by his boss Auchinleck and welcomed by the prime minister in London. Ritchie knew that Gott's command would now be the critical centre of the battle and so decided to transfer the 1st Armoured Division to XIII Corps. The division was ordered to hold the line Acroma–Knightsbridge. Norrie's corps was given the task of attempting to strike at the enemy's rear, with 7th Motor Brigade and 10th Indian Division clearing the El Adem area.

That day Rommel struck northwards with the 15. and 21.Panzer divisions passing either side of the Knightsbridge Box, fighting all the way against determined resistance from the 201st Guards Brigade and the remnants of the armour. By the end of the day the armoured brigades were down to just 50 cruisers and 20 infantry tanks and Knightsbridge was almost surrounded. The 201st Guards Brigade would soon go the way of the 150th Brigade unless it was pulled out. Gott appreciated the situation and ordered that the defensive box be abandoned that night and the 201st Guards Brigade withdrawn to the north-east to Tobruk. Continuing pressure by the Panzer forces pushed Lumsden's armour northwards to the area south of Acroma. Rommel tried that day to close his trap around the two infantry divisions

still in the Gazala Line by driving on to cut the coast road, but his tired troops could not get past the small defensive boxes around Eluet et Tamar.

This day of action and continuing tank losses was really the end for Eighth Army. Even Auchinleck was forced to agree that Rommel had defeated its armoured forces and that its armour was weaker than that of the enemy in quantity as well as quality. All that was left was to try to stave off the Axis advances and to salvage as much from the debacle as possible. Eighth Army's strategy was now one of survival.

The 201st Guards Brigade withdrew from Knightsbridge that night and with its departure one of the cornerstones of the British defence line disappeared. The area west of Acroma was now completely vulnerable and the two now-isolated infantry divisions of XIII Corps in the Gazala Line virtually cut off. It was now time that they too should begin to withdraw. Ritchie had decided that the two divisions, still relatively fresh in view of the sparse fighting they had undertaken since the start of the Gazala battle, would withdraw eastwards, but had not yet decided where to. The problem worrying him that day was, what was to be done with Tobruk?

Back in February, both Ritchie and Auchinleck had decided that if Rommel's offensive was successful, Tobruk should not be held. They would not accept a second siege of the port and the drain on resources that such an action would have. Strategy had therefore been shaped to avoid Eighth Army being manoeuvred into a position whereby Tobruk would be lost. Unfortunately, Eighth Army was in danger of being placed into just such a position by the enemy. Ritchie now had to decide whether the conclusions drawn in February were to be put into practice. The decision was clear: if it seemed likely that Rommel was in danger of getting to a point where he could invest the port effectively, then Tobruk was to be given up. It was almost too

The commander of Panzerarmee Afrika in his personal command SdKfz 250/3 car 'Grief'. Rommel was renowned for roaming the battlefield seeking out his junior commanders in the field to find out what was going on at the sharp end and urging them into action. (IWM, HU 16766)

big a decision for Ritchie to make, for the epic story of Tobruk's first siege had a profound effect on public morale at home and it was well known that Churchill wished the port to be held. Ritchie thought that a compromise might be achieved if he allowed a temporary investment in the event of a Rommel breakthrough, with a view to restoring the situation when the strength of Eighth Army had been rebuilt. If the coastal road could be kept open and the garrison in the port sustained by the great volume of supplies stored there, there was a great chance that such a siege could be lifted in a matter of weeks.

Ritchie now decided that the 1st South African and the 50th divisions would stage a withdrawal from the Gazala Line and retreat to the frontier where they would form a defence behind which the armour could regroup. He ordered that the pull-out should begin that night, 14 June. He also ordered that the supply dump at Belhamed should be destroyed as far as possible to prevent the enemy seizing its stores and its 5,700,000 litres of fuel. Ritchie then sent a signal to Auchinleck asking if he agreed with risking a temporary investment of Tobruk, but omitted informing the Commander-in-Chief that he had given orders for the two infantry divisions to withdraw to Egypt. There was then a period of confusion, for Ritchie's message crossed in transmission with one from Auchinleck

Auchinleck had believed that Ritchie's earlier decision that he would 'stand and fight' would not include any withdrawals from the battlefield. He believed that the losses suffered by Rommel's army meant that it was now close to exhaustion. The enemy could not be expected to carry out large-scale offensive operations indefinitely, especially as British intelligence suggested that he was very short of ammunition. The pace of his attack would be sure to ease in the near future. Auchinleck therefore gave firm instructions to the army commander that Tobruk must be held and that the enemy must not be allowed to invest it. There would be no evacuation from Tobruk and the line Acroma–El Adem–Bir Gubi must be held. Auchinleck was sure that after such a lengthy battle Rommel was not strong enough to take Tobruk, especially if Ritchie kept his army as mobile as possible and attacked him at every opportunity.

The two infantry divisions in the Gazala Line began their withdrawal during the evening of 14 June. Pienaar's 1st South African Division was told to pull back along the coastal route, through Tobruk and then make for the Egyptian border. Major-General Ramsden's 50th Division, located farther south in the line, was ordered to break out south-westwards through the Italian X Corpo then make its way southwards round Bir Hacheim and across the desert to the frontier. During the night of the move, the small garrisons holding the defended localities between the Gazala Line and Acroma were also to be withdrawn. Those in Acroma itself held on until completely surrounded on 18 June and then withdrew into the Tobruk perimeter.

The moves began in the late afternoon when all the reserves of food, water and fuel within the divisional areas were silently destroyed or rendered unusable. The South Africans were aided by a dust storm that blew up in the

early evening and helped to shield their movements. One by one the three brigades pulled out of their positions and trekked back across the desert to join the coast road and move eastwards. During the night the move eastwards was checked on certain routes by small groups of Germans and the South Africans were often forced to fight their way past. The main body of the enemy near Acroma did not pick up this movement until daylight the next day when they found that the troops facing them had disappeared. The division's rearguards had the worst of the evacuation with many of them being captured or scattered by the now roused enemy. During the retreat, 1st South African Division lost 27 men killed and 366 wounded or missing.

Major-General Ramsden's 50th Division had a much harder task. It was to break out in two main brigade groups. Each group was to use one battalion to create a gap in the Italian positions and then hold it open whilst the remainder of the brigade passed through. Late that afternoon a dust storm blew across their front just as the Italians were attacked. The ferocity and strength of the assault by both lead battalions quickly opened gaps and the following battalions braved Italian fire to storm through the breaches, overrun the enemy positions and gain the open desert in the rear. One battalion however, the 9th Durham Light Infantry, was delayed in starting out and ran into a welter of Italian fire that forced it back. The Durham's colonel, Lieutenant-Colonel Percy, decided that his battalion would take its chances by withdrawing to the rear and making for the coast road. Various stragglers joined his group and they fought their way back to Tobruk the next day through numerous German positions. By 16 June, the bulk of the division was assembling on the Egyptian frontier.

PHASE FOUR: THE LOSS OF TOBRUK

With the withdrawal of all forces west of Acroma, the British line now ran from Tobruk to El Adem and then out into the eastern desert. Eighth Army had been defeated and driven some 129km from its original lines and its defended localities had been reduced to just Tobruk itself, El Adem and Belhamed. Its armour consisted of one weak armoured brigade, the 4th; there were no complete infantry formations outside Tobruk and no appreciable reserves.

A postwar photograph of the anti-tank ditch between Tobruk and El Adem that formed part of the defences of the fortress area. (Steve Bulpit)

Ritchie planned for Lt. Gen. Gott's XIII Corps to deny Tobruk to the enemy whilst Lt. Gen. Norrie's XXX Corps conducted operations outside the port perimeter. Norrie would have under his command the 7th Armoured Division, containing the survivors of 4th Armoured and 7th Motor brigades, together with the 3rd Indian Motor Brigade, the 29th Indian Brigade at El Adem and the 20th Indian Brigade at Belhamed with which to prevent the enemy moving around the eastern side of Tobruk.

Rommel had detected large British troop movements eastwards on 15 June and reasoned that Ritchie was withdrawing the bulk of his forces to the Egyptian frontier. When he reported these facts back to his Italian superior, Maresciallo Bastico, he was told to continue with his attacks to retain the initiative in order to seize Tobruk. Axis forces could not again allow a long siege of the port to take place, as this would interfere with the agreed plan that the next operation in that theatre was to be the capture of Malta. All air forces were to be withdrawn from North Africa at the end of the month to take part in this attack. Nor would any more German reinforcements be sent to Rommel, as Hitler had banned the movement of troops by sea until after Malta had fallen.

Rommel did not need to be told what his next move should be for he was already determined to keep up the pressure on Eighth Army and immediately ordered a move eastwards by the Afrika Korps to try to cut off as many of the British as he could. The 21.Panzer Division was told to advance on Belhamed and the 90.leichte Division on El Adem.

Generalmajor Ulrich Kleeman's 90.leichte Division was the first to move and attacked the 29th Indian Brigade at El Adem late on 15 June. This attack and two others were beaten off that day, as was another by 21.Panzer Division on a defended locality at Point B650 eight kilometres to the north. Both of these attacks were repulsed with the help of 7th Motor Brigade, which left Norrie signalling to Ritchie that he thought El Adem would be able to hold fast.

He was wrong, for the next day the 21.Panzer Division overran Point B650 and closed on Belhamed. This left El Adem vulnerable and Norrie felt that little could be achieved by a last-ditch stand so gave orders for the 29th Indian Brigade to pull out and withdraw eastwards that night, 16/17 June. With El Adem in enemy hands, the southern cornerstone of the outward defences of Tobruk had gone. The loss of the defended locality also meant that the airfields around Gambut were under threat and Air Vice-Marshal Coningham gave orders for all aircraft based there to move 64km eastwards to Sidi Azeiz. This severely limited the amount of air support available to Eighth Army.

Next to fall was Belhamed, and this became untenable when the 21.Panzer Division was joined by 15.Panzer Division and the Afrika Korps were directed to drive for the sea near Gambut. The 4th Armoured Brigade clashed with these German tanks between El Adem and Belhamed on the afternoon of 17 June and, after a stiff engagement, withdrew south-east to an area near

Trig el Abd. It was then finally ordered back to the frontier with Egypt. Now, with no armoured protection or mobile forces to stem the German Panzers, the 20th Indian Brigade was ordered to withdraw from the Belhamed positions and retreat eastwards to Sollum during the night.

The 20th Indian Brigade did not get away unscathed, for that same night Rommel's armour reached the coast and cut part of its escape route. Two of its battalions, the 1st South Wales Borderers and the 3/18th Royal Garhwal Rifles, clashed with the enemy and were forced to scatter and try to get past the roadblocks. In this they were unsuccessful for virtually all of the escaping troops and their equipment were captured. With the flight of this Indian brigade Rommel had encircled the whole of Tobruk and cleared British troops from an area that extended 64km to the east. Tobruk was once again under siege and on its own.

With great delight Rommel reported to his masters in Berlin on 18 June that his forces had now invested the vital port of Tobruk. He also said that he wished to exploit the general disorganization and inevitable fall in morale of those defenders now holed up in Tobruk following the rout of the British. He called upon the Luftwaffe to give him all the aid it could to help capture the port area in as short a time as possible. Generalfeldmarschall Kesselring was anxious for attention now to be given to the capture of Malta, but agreed to employ as many of his aircraft as were available to concentrate on what was clearly a tempting target. Tobruk was close to the newly captured airfields at Gazala and El Adem and, with the RAF having been evicted to landing grounds away to the east, British opposition from the air was unlikely. (In fact on 19 June the Desert Air Force was forced to withdraw even farther eastwards from Sidi Azeiz to Sidi Barrani, which meant that it now had just one squadron of long-range Kittyhawks capable of giving any cover to the Tobruk garrison.) Kesselring now ordered every bomber unit in North Africa to take part in the attack and even transferred some aircraft from Crete and Greece for the operation.

Rommel intended to lose little time in capturing Tobruk for he was anxious to keep in contact with the retreating Eighth Army and take advantage of its demise. He gave orders that same day for the assault on

Eighth Army's withdrawal and Rommel's attack on Tobruk

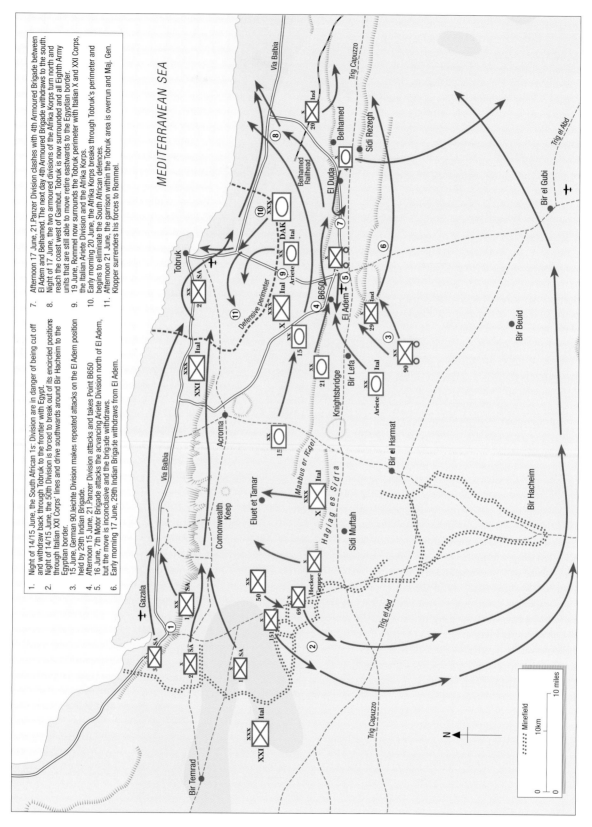

1. Night of 14/15 June, the South African 1s: Division are in danger of being cut off and withdraw back through Tobruk to the frontier with Egypt.
2. Night of 14/15 June, the 50th Division is forced to break out of its encircled positions through Italian XXI Corps' lines and drive southwards around Bir Hacheim to the Egyptian border.
3. 15 June, German 90.leichte Division makes repeated attacks on the El Adem position held by 29th Indian Brigade.
4. Afternoon 15 June, 21.Panzer Division attacks and takes Point B650.
5. 16 June, 7th Motor Brigade attacks the advancing Ariete Division north of El Adem, but the move is inconclusive and the brigade withdraws.
6. Early morning 17 June, 29th Indian Brigade withdraws from El Adem.
7. Afternoon 17 June, 21.Panzer Division clashes with 4th Armoured Brigade between El Adem and Belhamed. The next day 4th Armoured Brigade withdraws to the south.
8. Night of 17 June, the two armoured divisions of the Afrika Korps turn north and reach the coast west of Gambut. Tobruk is now surrounded and all Eighth Army units that are still able to move retire eastwards to the Egyptian border.
9. 19 June, Rommel now surrounds the Tobruk perimeter with Italian X and XXI Corps, the Italian Ariete Division and the Afrika Korps.
10. Early morning 20 June, the Afrika Korps breaks through Tobruk's perimeter and begins to eliminate the South African defences.
11. Afternoon 21 June, the garrison within the Tobruk area is overrun and Maj. Gen. Klopper surrenders his forces to Rommel.

76

An abandoned British anti-tank gun position on the outskirts of Tobruk after its capture by German troops. The stacks of ready-to-use ammunition show that the position had probably been quickly overwhelmed by the advancing mobile troops of the Afrika Korps. (IWM, MH5871)

Tobruk to begin early on 20 June. The Italian XXI and X corps, who were given the task of holding the western and southern sides of the boundary, joined his forces in a continuous ring around the perimeter of the defended area. The Italian 132ᵃ Divisione Corazzata 'Ariete' held the south-east corner and the Afrika Korps the eastern side. The 90.leichte and the 'Trieste' divisions were farther to the east keeping watch and maintaining contact with Eighth Army.

At the same time that Rommel was informing Berlin that his forces had once again surrounded Tobruk, Auchinleck was receiving the news that Belhamed had been given up and that his only armour in contact with the enemy, the 4th Armoured Brigade, had been defeated and had retired into the desert. As late as 2200hrs the previous evening he was signalling to Ritchie to hold the line at El Adem and to counterattack when a suitable opportunity presented itself. Ritchie signalled to the Commander-in-Chief that he was finding it difficult to comply with these requests and Auchinleck flew up to Ritchie's headquarters at Maddalena to discuss the matter.

What Gen. Auchinleck found was that a complete disaster had overtaken Ritchie's command. Tobruk was surrounded, Eighth Army had been virtually evicted from Libya and the employment of a force capable of mounting any counterattack was just wishful thinking. Auchinleck decided to place the defence of Tobruk directly under Army Headquarters, with XIII Corps responsible for defending the frontier and the area to the west, and XXX Corps sent into general reserve in the area of Matruh where it would re-form and train a new strike force ready for the renewal of offensive action.

The Tobruk of June 1942 was not the same fortress that had endured the long siege of the previous year; its defences were in a very poor state. The neglect was caused by a number of factors, the most significant of which was Auchinleck's February decision that it was not to be held if surrounded. The success of the *Crusader* offensive the previous winter and its use as a major supply base for the proposed spring offensive into Tripolitania all diverted attention away from regarding the port area as a stronghold. Many of its protective minefields and wire had been cleared for use in the Gazala Line and

Among the first German troops in Tobruk, were this medical team from the Afrika Korps, who are happy to pose for the photographer. Their light personnel vehicle is an MV2, a type that was widely used throughout the German Army. The capture of the port and fortress area was a great coup for the Axis and earned Rommel his *Generalfeldmarschall*'s baton. (IWM, MH5856)

some of the anti-tank ditches around the perimeter had collapsed or been filled in. Now, with the suddenness of Rommel's advance and the breakdown of Eighth Army's protective screen, Tobruk was again in the front line and its long 48km perimeter was in great need of its fortress reputation.

The troops garrisoning Tobruk were drawn from a variety of formations and consisted of two brigades from the 2nd South African Division, the 201st Guards Motor Brigade Group and the 11th Indian Brigade, together with the 61 Valentine and Matilda infantry tanks of the 32nd Army Tank Brigade. Despite having two landing grounds within the defences, there were no aircraft available, nor were there very many anti-aircraft guns with which to deter the Luftwaffe. One thing that was in abundance, however, was the enormous quantity of supplies. There were three million rations to sustain the 35,000 men of the garrison, along with 7,000 tons of water, one and a half million gallons of fuel and nearly 300,000 rounds of field, medium, anti-tank and anti-aircraft ammunition for the three field regiments, two medium regiments, one anti-tank battery and one anti-aircraft battery of artillery within the defences.

Auchinleck placed a South African, Maj. Gen. H. B. Klopper, in command of all forces within the perimeter. Klopper was a general with little battle experience who had come from a training command to take over the 2nd South African Division just one month previously. At his first conference with his subordinates on 18 June, Klopper declared that Tobruk would be held as part of Eighth Army's wider plan and he asked them to be prepared for a siege of at least three months. Klopper proved to be a headstrong individual who chose to ignore the advice of his more experienced junior commanders on a number of important matters regarding the defence of Tobruk, including those of Brigadier Willison who had served through the earlier siege as commander of the garrison's reserve.

Tobruk was more than a defended port in the eyes of the British public, and indeed those of the free world. The siege of the previous year and Eighth Army's successful lifting of that blockade during Operation *Crusader* had given public morale a huge boost and reinforced the belief that the defeat of Nazi Germany and ultimate victory in the war was assured. The tenacity

A German Kübelwagen parks close by some of the thousands of British and South African troops captured by Panzerarmee Afrika when the fortress area of Tobruk fell. (IWM, MH5880)

of the resistance of those trapped inside and the heroic support from the Royal Navy and Royal Air Force was the stuff of legends. Failure to hold Tobruk and restore the initiative to the British Army would be unthinkable.

On 20 June, there was a feeling within Tobruk that Rommel's main forces had swept on eastwards after the tail of Eighth Army. In fact, during the darkness of the previous night Rommel had brought the Afrika Korps round to face the eastern perimeter of the fortress ready for an assault. At 0520hrs a massed artillery bombardment fell on the south-eastern corner of the compound and was soon joined by a sustained attack by Axis aircraft and dive-bombers. Just before 0700hrs German infantry crept forwards and began their assault on the outer defences, giving cover to the engineers who moved up to make crossings of the anti-tank ditch. Within an hour breaches had been made and tanks had crossed over the obstacles, through the minefields and wire, and were dealing with the main British defences.

Both the 15. and 21.Panzer divisions urged their total of 90-plus tanks through the gaps before the British armour could react. Over to their left the 132ª Divisione Corazzata 'Ariete' was also attempting its own break-in. It was almost 1000hrs before British tanks reached the area of the Axis assault and clashed with the German armour. For a while this intervention helped the infantry resist the enemy around the inner defensive position. So successful were they that a report was passed on to Klopper that the situation was in hand. Shortly before midday the state of affairs changed dramatically when the two Panzer divisions launched a strong attack and broke through the last defensive barrier. Within an hour German tanks had pushed aside most of

the tanks of 32nd Army Tank Brigade and were closing on an area of higher ground termed 'Kings Cross' – the junction of the roads to El Adem and Bardia. By 1400hrs the 21.Panzer Division was just eight kilometres from the harbour and shelling the town.

By the end of the afternoon Rommel had tanks in Tobruk itself with infantry starting to mop up British resistance and prevent any escapees embarking from the port. A great swathe had been cut into the Tobruk fortress area and parties of Germans and Italians were clearing out British positions throughout the eastern side of the defensive zone. The commander of No. 88 Sub-Area in charge of all the supply dumps, Brigadier Thompson, watched the enemy drawing closer and obtained permission from the commanding general to begin the demolition of all supplies under his command. Fires were lit, equipment blown up and great oil tanks set ablaze, sending a plume of black smoke skywards over the doomed fortress.

The 15.Panzer Division had meanwhile moved westwards along the Pilastrino Ridge and was closing on Maj. Gen. Klopper's headquarters located at the end of the ridge in Fort Pilastrino. At around 1600hrs Klopper's staff sighted these tanks and the general concluded that his headquarters would be overrun in a matter of minutes. He ordered his staff to destroy all documents and equipment and to disperse. The signal office and telephone exchange and virtually all of the radio sets were demolished. At the last moment, the tanks moved away, directed to the south-west and the rear of the untouched British defences. Klopper now decided to set up a command post at the 6th South African Brigade's headquarters in the north-western end of the fortress, but was now hampered in exercising command by the previous destruction and dispersal of his own headquarters.

Klopper decided that a stand would be made in the western area of the fortress on the ground still held by South African troops who had not been seriously attacked. By 2000hrs he had changed his mind and concluded that an effective defence was impossible. He signalled to all units that they should prepare for a mass breakout starting during the night. This order was given to mobile troops at around 0200hrs the next day and some transport attempted to get out of the fortress and away to the west. Those without transport, which was most of the garrison, had no hope of escape. Klopper signalled to Ritchie at Army HQ that his troops would 'resist to the last man and last round'. As the official history of the campaign later explained, 'this decision was approved by most of his subordinates but viewed with misgiving by some.'

Between 0500hrs and 0600hrs that morning Maj. Gen. Klopper changed his mind and decided that little could now be achieved through further prolonged resistance. A short time later he sent out an officer to contact the enemy and ask for terms. By mid-morning orders had been received by all units to cease firing and to lay down their arms. Tobruk had surrendered. The fortress that had previously withstood siege for seven months had resisted for just one day.

This order was received with general amazement by many and disbelief by a few. The 2nd/7th Gurkha rifles and the 2nd Cameron Highlanders refused to surrender and fought on, with the Gurkhas resisting enemy attempts to stop them until 22 June. Another group of 199 men from the 2nd Coldstream Guards, led by Maj. Sainthill, fought their way out and escaped back to Egypt, collecting a further 188 stragglers from other units along the way. Another small party of the Kaffrarian Rifles trekked along the coast on foot, dodging parties of Germans and Italians to reach the British lines at El Alamein 38 days later.

The loss of Tobruk was a great disaster for the British; over 33,000 British, South African, Indian and native troops were taken into captivity along with vast amounts of stores, fuel and ammunition. So swift was the collapse that the planned destruction of these supplies could not be put into operation. Most discouraging was that over 2,000 serviceable vehicles were seized and put into use by the Axis forces. Nor was the disaster just measured in human and material terms, the blow to British and South African pride and morale was incalculable – South Africa had lost a third of all its forces in the field.

Winston Churchill was in Washington when news of the surrender reached him, humiliatingly handed over whilst in a meeting with President Roosevelt. He felt that it was one of the heaviest blows he had received during the war. Further embarrassment was heaped upon him when a motion expressing no confidence in the direction of the war was tabled in the House of Commons. The mood of the nation was at a very low ebb.

The gloom that descended over Eighth Army was in great contrast to the pride and triumph felt by all of Rommel's Panzerarmee Afrika. Recognition and admiration for this victorious force and its charismatic commander rang around the world. In Berlin, Rommel's bold and devastating conquest of the whole of Libya and the thrashing of Eighth Army led to his immediate promotion to *Generalfeldmarschall*. He instantly became Germany's most famous and successful general. He now looked for further triumphs and another clash with British Eighth Army in Egypt.

AFTERMATH

The capture of Tobruk was the end of the Gazala offensive that had begun on 26 May, but Panzerarmee Afrika did not pause to savour this victory. Eighth Army was in retreat and Rommel was a general who always exploited his enemy's weaknesses. 'Press on' was his watchword, and press on he did, driving his force all out for the Egyptian border. But this was as far as his orders allowed him to go.

It had been agreed between Mussolini and Hitler on 1 May that Operation *Herkules*, the invasion of Malta, would take place following the capture of Tobruk. After Rommel's success against the British, Mussolini was still pushing for Malta to be occupied, but Hitler was having second thoughts; he felt that the island could become a further drain on resources. He was suspicious that the Italians would be of little help in taking the island and the operation would be, like the North African campaign, another mainly German venture. Besides, Rommel was pushing to be allowed to carry on eastwards and Hitler was inclined to agree with him.

In a message to Hitler, the new *Generalfeldmarschall* explained that as he had fulfilled the first part of his instructions – to defeat the enemy's army in the field and take Tobruk – he should now be allowed to continue with the chase without pause while such a favourable situation presented itself. He

A British Morris C8 truck, captured during the collapse of Tobruk and put back into service by the Germans. (IWM, MH5574)

had, he reasoned, captured large quantities of supplies, fuel and transport and the morale of his troops was in great shape. If he could now be given permission to continue and not to allow the enemy time to regroup and reinforce, he was sure he could pursue Eighth Army deep into Egypt and reach the Suez Canal and even the naval port of Alexandria.

Troops mounted in Bren carriers from the 9th Rifle Brigade watch the destruction of a supply dump from a distance during their retreat from the Gazala Line to new positions at El Alamein in Egypt. (IWM, E14010)

Hitler agreed with this logic and wrote to Mussolini supporting Rommel's request. 'A beaten army should always be pursued and completely destroyed', he urged. He then went on to explain that a great opportunity had presented itself that might not occur again. Mussolini was attracted to the idea of reaching the Suez Canal and evicting the British from North Africa and gave his consent for the advance to continue without pause. Malta would still be a problem, but if both his air force and the Luftwaffe concentrated all available air power against the island, then perhaps Malta could be neutralized as an offensive outpost of the British. It was a tempting prospect and on 25 June Mussolini sent the Commando Supremo, Maresciallo Ugo Cavallero, to meet with Kesselring and give the go-ahead for an advance into Egypt at least up to the El Alamein Line. Two days later this directive was extended to include the Suez Canal.

British strategy was also changing at this time. It had originally been decided to make a halt at the Egyptian frontier while a mobile force was reconstituted in the rear ready to strike at the enemy if he should penetrate or outflank the defences. Ritchie now thought that his scratch force of armour could never be regrouped and replenished before Rommel reached the border and resumed his attack. Any breakthrough by the enemy would be unlikely to be turned back. He therefore proposed withdrawing the bulk of Eighth Army to Matruh, 129km further to the east, and to make a stand there. Sufficient troops were to be left on the border to delay the Axis advance whilst others came forwards from bases farther east to Matruh. Auchinleck agreed that this was probably the best course of action in the circumstances.

Ritchie left Lt. Gen. Gott's XIII Corps to hold the frontier with the 7th Armoured, 50th and the 10th Indian divisions. The 1st South African Division was thought to be in need of retraining and was send on eastwards to the El Alamein Line to reorganize. Gott and Ritchie tried to decide between them just how long XIII Corps should hold on at the frontier, but events overtook any decision before it could be formalized.

Rommel had lost no time in chasing after Eighth Army. The 90.leichte Division had remained in contact with British stragglers and was soon joined by the Afrika Korps to become a once-again powerful mobile formation. The day after Tobruk had fallen, German troops reached and began crossing the frontier. The delaying action at the border proposed by Ritchie soon became an organized withdrawal as enemy forces quickly penetrated the scratch defences thrown up by the British. The frontier itself was no barrier to Rommel's eastward procession and Gott's forces pulled out at speed and headed back to the main body of Eighth Army at Matruh. It seemed that nothing could stop the German commander and his victorious forces.

The farther east the Axis army advanced, the closer it came to British airfields and advanced landing grounds. The RAF had been increasing in strength through new arrivals and quicker repairs as the front drew closer to its major bases and maintenance fields. Attacks by the Desert Air Force now increased dramatically, which was in stark contrast to the lessening of efforts by the Luftwaffe as Rommel's advance drew away from their bases. British aircraft now had clearly defined targets spread out along all roads and tracks leading east and their attacks began to seriously hurt the enemy.

As the British withdrew eastwards they continued their policy of demolitions and the destruction of all supply dumps, railway facilities and water points. Rommel advanced without opposition, but also without any replenishment of vital supplies from Eighth Army sources. Every kilometre east he travelled was one more kilometre over which each single item he needed to keep Panzerarmee Afrika in action had to be trucked forwards.

MERSA MATRUH

Ritchie and Auchinleck knew that Rommel had to be stopped and had decided to fight a decisive action at Matruh. The position was not ideal, but there were still some defensive positions from previous fighting around the port of Mersa Matruh itself and across the desert inland. Minefields had been laid from the sea to the two escarpments that ran parallel to the coast some 16 and 24km inland. Astride the second of these escarpments, some 16km east of the minefields was a planned position at Sidi Hamza, although because of the hard rock little effective work had been completed before the enemy arrived.

In the days following the collapse of Tobruk, new formations had been arriving to bolster Eighth Army. The Headquarters of X Corps, under the command of Lieutenant-General W. G. Holmes, had been moved from Syria and now came forwards to Matruh to relieve HQ XXX Corps. Norrie was now to take his HQ XXX Corps back to the rear at the El Alamein position to collect and organize a reserve strike force. Also arriving was the New Zealand Division, under the command of Lieutenant-General Bernard Freyberg VC, and the 10th Armoured Division. The 10th Armoured Division

was as yet untried in battle, so when it arrived in the Delta its 8th Armoured Brigade was stripped of all of its tanks to re-equip 1st Armoured Division and its men were returned to Cairo.

Ritchie's plans to defend the Matruh position had been hurriedly compiled between 22 and 24 June: X Corps was to hold Matruh and the coastal sector whilst XIII Corps held Sidi Hamza and the inland escarpments. Lieutenant-General Holmes's X Corps would have 10th Indian Division at Matruh, with 50th Division 16km to the south-east around Gerawla. Inland, XIII Corps would have 5th Indian Division around Sidi Hamza, the New Zealand Division eight kilometres to the rear at Minqar Qaim and the 1st Armoured Division, now containing both of 7th Armoured Division's armoured brigades, in the open desert 16km to the south-west. The 7th Armoured Division itself would use its 7th Motor Brigade and 3rd Indian Motor Brigade as a covering force to the extreme south of the line. The 29th Indian Brigade from 5th Indian Division, was also to provide two mobile detachments, 'Leathercol' and 'Gleecol', to operate between the two escarpments and to cover the narrowest part of the minefields. The intention was that Rommel's forces were to be held in front of Matruh and Sidi Hamza. In the event of a breakthrough between these positions or by a wide wheeling movement around to the south, his mobile forces were to be struck in the flank by the armour of XIII Corps.

The recent string of failures suffered by Eighth Army had hit morale hard. The superiority in numbers it had just a month before had been squandered; tank losses had reduced its armoured brigades to just scratch formations, cobbled together from repaired tanks or those taken from other units, and each attempt to halt the inexorable advance by the Afrika Korps had degenerated into chaos. The enemy was now inside Egypt and closing on the Nile Delta and all of its important cities, ports and installations. If Rommel could not be halted at Matruh, there was only the unfinished and poorly prepared El Alamein Line left on which to stop him. The situation looked bleak for the British, but Ritchie was determined to stay at Matruh. This time there would be no retreat; Eighth Army would stay there alive or dead.

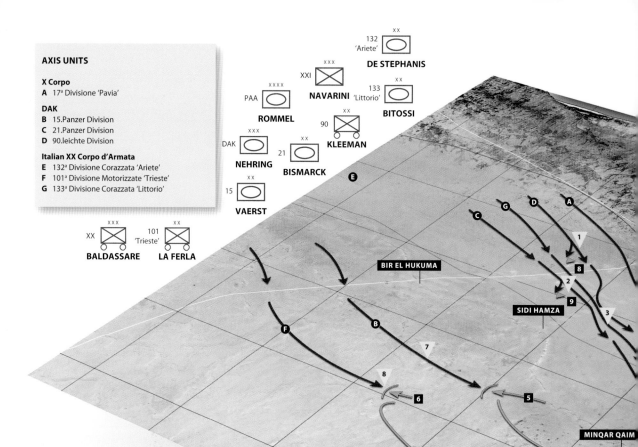

AXIS UNITS

X Corpo
A 17ª Divisione 'Pavia'

DAK
B 15.Panzer Division
C 21.Panzer Division
D 90.leichte Division

Italian XX Corpo d'Armata
E 132ª Divisione Corazzata 'Ariete'
F 101ª Divisione Motorizzate 'Trieste'
G 133ª Divisione Corazzata 'Littorio'

132 'Ariete' — **DE STEPHANIS**
XXI **NAVARINI**
PAA **ROMMEL**
133 'Littorio' — **BITOSSI**
90 **KLEEMAN**
DAK **NEHRING**
21 **BISMARCK**
15 **VAERST**
E

BALDASSARE 101 'Trieste' **LA FERLA**

BIR EL HUKUMA
SIDI HAMZA
MINQAR QAIM

EVENTS

1 Late afternoon 26 June, the 90.leichte Division advances between the two ridges and overcomes the 'Leathercol' mobile column in its path.

2 Late afternoon 26 June, the 21.Panzer Division moves through the minefield and attacks the 'Gleecol' mobile column.

3 The 21.Panzer and 90.leichte divisions halt for the night.

4 First light 27 June, the 90.leichte Division advances to Bir Sarahna on the northern ridge, but is held by the 151st Brigade of 50th Division.

5 The 21.Panzer Division advances to Minqar Qaim where it is shelled by artillery of the New Zealand Division.

6 The Italian 133ª Divisione Corazzata 'Littorio' follows 21.Panzer Division and advances to Bir Shineina where it is held up by artillery fire.

7 The 15.Panzer Division drives to the south of the southern ridge where it is confronted and held by 22nd Armoured Brigade of 1st Armoured Division.

8 The 101ª Divisione Motorizzate 'Trieste' advances on the right of 15.Panzer Division and is confronted by 4th Armoured Brigade, which has been attached to 1st Armoured Division.

9 The 5th Indian Brigade of 10th Indian Division comes south from Matruh in an attempt to strike the flank of the Afrika Korps, but is held on the northern ridge by the Italian 17ª Divisione 'Pavia'.

10 Rommel arrives on the battlefield and orders 90.leichte Division to drive eastwards and then northwards to cut the coastal road in the rear of British X Corps.

11 The 21.Panzer Division attempts to encircle the New Zealand Division's positions, but is prevented by tanks of 1st Armoured Division.

12 Late evening 27 June, the 69th and 151st brigades of 50th Division attack southwards to hit Rommel's forces in the flank, but are unable to gain the northern ridge.

13 Late evening 27 June, the tanks of 1st Armoured Division disengage and withdraw to the east.

14 The New Zealand Division breaks out of its positions through 21.Panzer Division and withdraws to the east.

15 Nightfall 27 June, 21.Panzer Division sends units eastwards chasing XIII Corps' formations.

16 28 June, the isolated divisions of Lt. Gen. Holmes' X Corps make preparations to break out. Later, during the hours of darkness, the 10th Indian Division and British 50th Division fight their way through the enemy positions into the desert before turning east and racing to safety.

THE ACTION AT MATRUH 26–28 JUNE 1942
Auchinleck fights a delaying action before withdrawing to the El Alamein Line.

Note: Gridlines are shown at intervals of 10 km/6.21 miles

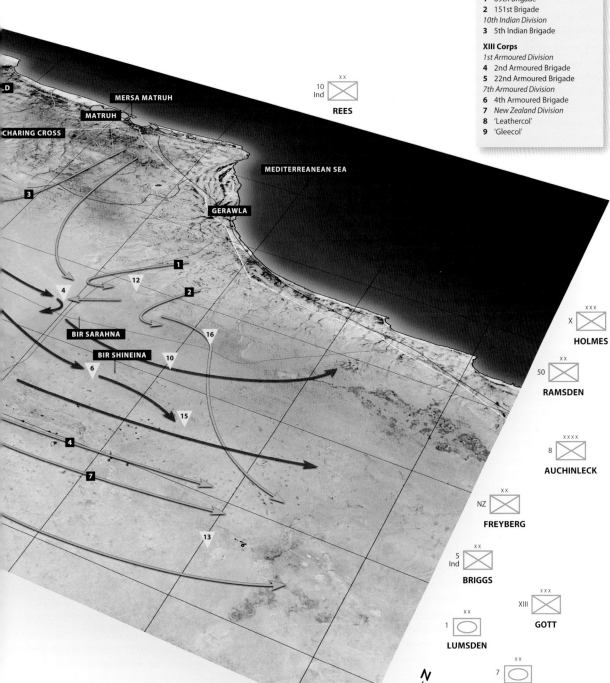

BRITISH UNITS

X Corps
50th Division
1 69th Brigade
2 151st Brigade
10th Indian Division
3 5th Indian Brigade

XIII Corps
1st Armoured Division
4 2nd Armoured Brigade
5 22nd Armoured Brigade
7th Armoured Division
6 4th Armoured Brigade
7 New Zealand Division
8 'Leathercol'
9 'Gleecol'

10 Ind REES

MERSA MATRUH

MATRUH

CHARING CROSS

MEDITERREANEAN SEA

GERAWLA

X HOLMES

50 RAMSDEN

8 AUCHINLECK

NZ FREYBERG

5 Ind BRIGGS

XIII GOTT

1 LUMSDEN

7 MESSERVY

BIR SARAHNA

BIR SHINEINA

N

87

General Auchinleck talks to a lieutenant-colonel from 50th Division on the coastal Via Balbia during the great retreat from Gazala to El Alamein. (IWM, E13889)

As Commander-in-Chief Middle East, Gen. Auchinleck knew better than most just how bad things were. The position of Eighth Army and indeed the whole security of Egypt were in great danger of being overwhelmed. Auchinleck decided that the situation was so serious he would take command in the field. On 25 June he relieved Lt. Gen. Ritchie as the head of Eighth Army and placed himself in control. The previous position, whereby Ritchie was titular head of Eighth Army but consulted Auchinleck on virtually every matter, had clearly not worked. Ritchie had originally moved from a staff post at Auchinleck's HQ into a position of command at the head of Britain's most important army without any experience at this higher level. He was in fact much less experienced than many of his subordinate commanders. Probably because of this, he was not able to impose his own will on them. In contrast, Rommel commanded his forces with a very firm hand and forceful personality, allowing no compromise or variation from his strict orders. But then Ritchie was no Rommel and it showed. It would have no doubt been better for Eighth Army if Auchinleck had made this move much sooner.

Those troops moving into the makeshift positions around Matruh still had the sting of defeat about them. They were not in the best of spirits for they knew that the enemy was approaching and the situation at Matruh was still short of being ready to absorb the full force of Panzerarmee Afrika when it arrived. The confusion that went with sudden collapse and a speedy retreat affected the organization of all formations. New arrivals and reinforcements added to this confusion, as did the takeover by HQ X Corps of XXX Corps' sector of the line. To all this was added a change of command at the top, a change of plan and a new approach to the business of fighting.

Auchinleck was thinking hard about his present strategy; perhaps the do-or-die attitude that Ritchie had proclaimed was not necessarily the right one. He knew that he could not really afford to be pinned down at Matruh and have his forces defeated in detail. If Eighth Army lost a decisive battle here at Matruh it would be the end of Egypt and perhaps the whole of the Middle East. On the other hand, so long as Eighth Army remained as a force there would always be hope. Ritchie's plan was a continuation of all the previous attempts to stop Rommel and now Auchinleck decided to change that.

Early in the morning of 26 June Auchinleck issued fresh orders to his corps commanders. The new leader of Eighth Army decided that he would no longer attempt to fight a decisive action at Matruh. He intended to engineer a running battle with Rommel over a large area between Matruh and the El Alamein Line. All of Eighth Army's forces were to be kept mobile and to strike at the enemy from all sides. The tanks were not to be committed unless they were in a favourable position. If ground has to be given up, then so be it. The most important policy now was to keep the army together; there was no longer to be any static forces holding localities that could be surrounded and isolated from the main force. Auchinleck insisted that each division reorganize itself into brigade battlegroups based on their artillery units, capable of hitting hard and staying fluid. Of course there was not enough transport for all brigades to be converted in this way, so the remainder of each division was to be sent back to the Alamein position.

Before any of these changes could be put into place, Rommel's forces arrived at the Matruh position after a delayed advance caused by fuel shortages and round-the-clock air attacks. They immediately launched a probing attack. The 90.leichte Division advanced in the centre between the two escarpments after having crossed the narrow minefields of the outer defence line and scattered the 'Leathercol' mobile force guarding the area between the two features. The 21.Panzer Division advancing on its right did likewise to the 'Gleecol' column. Once through the minefields, the two divisions stopped for the night.

Rommel's plan of attack was for 90.leichte Division to drive between the escarpments and cut the coast road to the east of Matruh to isolate the port and town area. The Afrika Korps would advance either side of the southern ridge, with the 21.Panzer Division to the north and the 15.Panzer Division to the south. The Italian X and XXI corps would contain the Matruh area and Italian XX Corpo would advance behind 15.Panzer Division.

Early on 27 June the attack resumed with 90.leichte Division advancing as far as Bir Sarahna below Minqar Qaim. Here the division ran into a battalion of the Durham Light Infantry from 50th Division's 151st Brigade and was halted by determined resistance and artillery fire. The two divisions of the Afrika Korps were also checked in their advance by strong forces along the southern escarpment. Rommel now had his force strung out between two British corps and was for a moment vulnerable. A counterattack by 5th Indian Brigade into the rear of 90.leichte Division failed to make any appreciable progress, but a flank attack on 15.Panzer Division, now supported by the 101ª Divisione Motorizzate 'Trieste', by 4th and 22nd armoured brigades did manage to halt the southern group of the enemy for a while.

On the other side of the southern escarpment 21.Panzer Division came under heavy fire from the New Zealand Division, the presence of which was unknown to Rommel. By early afternoon the enemy attack was beginning to slow down. At around this time Rommel himself arrived on the battlefield and got the 90.leichte Division going again, telling their commander Kleeman that he had to cut the coastal road that night. Meanwhile the 21.Panzer Division had manoeuvred into a position whereby it was able to attack the New Zealand Division from the north and the east. The attacks were held without too much difficulty, but the Germans continued to move around the

Eighth Army's retreat to the El Alamein Line

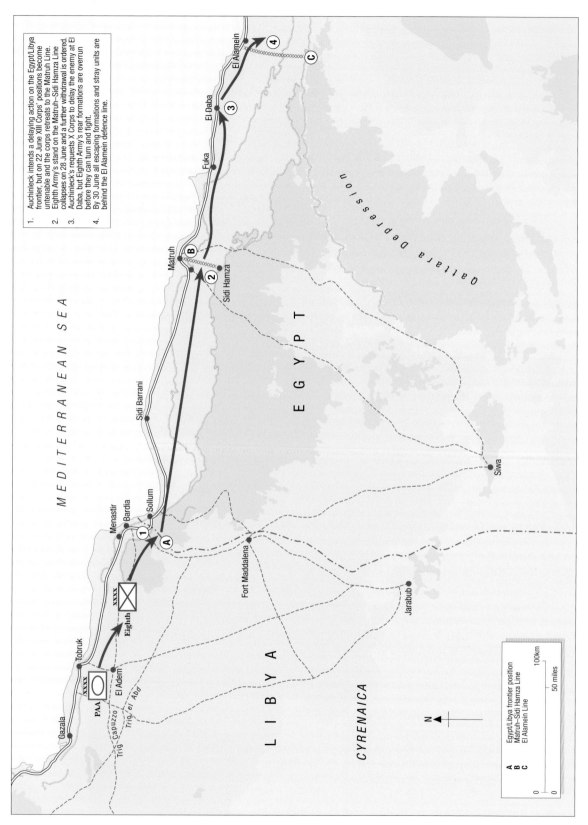

1. Auchinleck intends a delaying action on the Egypt/Libya frontier, but on 22 June XIII Corps' positions become untenable and the corps retreats to the Matruh Line.
2. Eighth Army's stand on the Matruh–Sidi Hamza Line collapses on 28 June and a further withdrawal is ordered.
3. Auchinleck's requests X Corps to delay the enemy at El Daba, but Eighth Army's rear formations are overrun before they can turn and fight.
4. By 30 June all escaping formations and stray units are behind the El Alamein defence line.

A	Egypt/Libya frontier position
B	Matruh–Sidi Hamza Line
C	El Alamein Line

high ground and threatened the division's transport on the southern side of the escarpment. The situation improved when tanks from 1st Armoured Division came to the aid of the New Zealanders and forced the Panzer division to halt its attack, but the armour was told not to remain in contact for too long.

At Auchinleck's headquarters the messages coming in from all positions told of heavy and confused fighting. It was difficult for the army commander to have a clear picture of what was happening, although it did seem that the enemy had made large and threatening penetrations of the line. Auchinleck's previous instructions that no formation was to be isolated and ground was to be given up if necessary rather than risk being surrounded, allowed great freedom of action to his corps commanders. With the New Zealanders being threatened on three sides, Lt. Gen. Gott saw his corps in danger of being split. He had already given instructions that if a withdrawal was ordered his three divisions were to fall back to a position in front of Fuka and now signalled his intention to do so that night. A second stage of the withdrawal was intended to take them back to El Alamein.

With Auchinleck agreeing to XIII Corps' pulling out, it was necessary to inform X Corps to do likewise, but communications between Eighth Army and Lt. Gen. Holmes's command failed and X Corps was not aware that the withdrawal was to take place that night. In the meantime, Holmes continued with a proposed counterattack into the flanks of Rommel's forces.

The situation in the New Zealand Division took a turn for the worse in the early evening when its commander, Maj. Gen. Freyberg VC, was wounded and evacuated from the battlefield. His place was taken by Brigadier L. Inglis of 4th New Zealand Brigade. Inglis felt that as the division was almost surrounded and its guns were down to just a few rounds of ammunition it had to pull out as soon as possible. At 1920hrs permission to do just that was given by Gott, although there was some confusion in Inglis's mind where he was to withdraw to. A garbled message suggested that it was right back to the Alamein Line. When the New Zealand Division started to move out it found its way blocked by 21.Panzer Division and so it was compelled to fight its way out. This it did with great violence and speed, bursting through the German positions and inflicting much shock and discomfort to the enemy. It then continued its move to the east and never stopped until it was inside the positions along the Alamein Line. Gott's other two divisions disengaged themselves that night and fell back to the Fuka position.

Over in X Corps' sector, Holmes continued with his southwards counterattack into Rommel's flank, but his troops were unable to reach the first escarpment. In the early evening he heard the discomfiting news that the enemy had cut the coast road at Gerawla and isolated his corps from the rest of Eighth Army. It was not until the next morning that contact was resumed with army HQ and he found out that Gott's corps had pulled out. Auchinleck told Holmes that his corps was to slip out that night with the whole of his force on a broad front, then turn east on the high ground and rally at El Daba, 97km away between Fuka and El Alamein.

RETREAT TO EL ALAMEIN

For the rest of 28 June the 50th and 5th Indian divisions held their lines against slight opposition whilst the enemy pushed on eastwards and made contact with XIII Corps in Fuka. That night the two divisions broke out and

German War Cemetery near Tobruk built in the shape of a Crusader castle. (Steve Bulpit)

attacked southwards for 48km then turned eastwards and sped across the desert intermingling with enemy units and supply lines in a dash for safety. Virtually every column fought a running battle along the way and lost numbers of men and vehicles. Lieutenant-General Holmes and his headquarters had to run the gauntlet just like every other unit, bursting their way forwards through groups of Germans and Italians. Their passage became even worse at Fuka where the enemy were already engaged by the rearguard of XIII Corps. At El Daba there was no time to regroup, for by then all of Eighth Army was on the move trying to get back into some sort of refuge at El Alamein

By 30 June all those units that were capable of escaping were back behind the Alamein Line. Auchinleck had withdrawn his army into what was now very much the last-ditch position. It was disorganized, exhausted and confused, but it was intact and with a framework of command on which it could be rebuilt to its former strength. To its rear were great quantities of supplies, fuel and reinforcements. Above it in the sky, the Desert Air Force was present in strength, flying from airfields close by. Auchinleck's army was certainly down, but it was not yet completely beaten.

A few miles to the west, already in contact with the Alamein positions, were the forward troops of Rommel's Afrika Korps. They were also exhausted, but renewal and replenishment was unlikely for these tired formations, for they had stretched their lines of supply and communication virtually to breaking point. They had outrun their air cover, used virtually all of their fuel and ammunition and had run their tanks into the ground. Rommel was pressing them on, but, like the British just a few miles away, they were in no fit state to launch what could be the decisive battle of the campaign. Two tired armies now looked at each other across the desert at El Alamein and prepared for what was to be the final showdown.

THE BATTLEFIELD TODAY

The Libyan battlefield of May and June 1942 is no more than wide tracts of desert sand and rock, with few recognizable landmarks and virtually no features of any kind. Actions were fought to command map references rather than hills, towns or rivers as is normal in war. The fluid nature of this period of armoured warfare often meant that successive battles took place over the same terrain again and again with the purpose of wiping out as much of the enemy's force as possible.

As with other North African battlefields, the remoteness of the barren landscape results in few outsiders visiting the area and it is therefore likely that unexploded ordnance, especially mines, remain scattered over the region. For this reason any visit to the Gazala district should be as part of an organized group led by guides who have an intimate knowledge of the ground.

Libya itself is just now becoming more accessible after a long period during which it was at odds with western countries. For the moment a person wishing to study the battlefield at first hand would be best advised to travel with one of the battlefield tour operators who regularly visit North Africa. These companies and their tours can be found listed on various Internet sites.

British War cemetery at Tobruk. (Commonwealth War Graves Commission)

FURTHER READING AND BIBLIOGRAPHY

Two books stand out as a source for further study of the Gazala battles. First, the volume of the British Official History that deals with the period, Major-General Playfair's *The Mediterranean and Middle East Volume III*, and, second, Barrie Pitt's *The Crucible of War: Auchinleck's Command*. These two books complement each other by providing factual details of the commanders, the units, the actions and the outcome of the battles, with more intimate and personal appreciations of the fighting, the personalities involved, together with the experiences and the disappointments of the men who fought the battle.

For details of Rommel's forces, I would recommend the work of that great armoured historian George Forty and his boook *The Armies of Rommel*. A very sound analysis of the decision-making behind the scenes in Eighth Army during this crisis of British command is Michael Carver's *Dilemmas of the Desert War*. Rommel's thoughts and opinions are laid out in *The Rommel Papers* edited by Basil Liddell Hart, a book that is invaluable to anyone interested in the North African campaign. Finally, although this list could be expanded to ten times its size, I would recommend another of Basil Liddell Hart's books, *The Tanks: The History of the Royal Tank Regiment, Volume Two* for its intimate account of the units from the RTR that took part in the fighting in Libya.

Anon, *The Tiger Kills*, HMSO: London, 1944

Braddock, D. W., *The Campaigns in Egypt and Libya 1940–1942*, Gale and Polden: Aldershot, 1964

Carver, Michael, *Dilemmas of the Desert War: The Libyan Campaign 1940–1942*, Batsford: London, 1986

Clay, Maj. Ewart, *The Path of the 50th*, Gale and Polden: Aldershot, 1950

Delaney, John, *Fighting the Desert Fox*, Arms and Armour: London, 1998

Forty, George, *The Armies of Rommel*, Arms and Armour: London, 1997

Fraser, David, *Knight's Cross: The Life of Field Marshal Erwin Rommel*, Harper Collins: London, 1993

Irving, David, *The Trail of the Fox: The Life of Field Marshal Erwin Rommel*, Weidenfeld and Nicholson: London, 1977

Joslen, Lt. Col. H. F., *Orders of Battle: Second World War 1939–1945*, HMSO London, 1960

Liddell Hart, Capt. B. H. (ed), *The Rommel Papers*, Collins: London, 1953

Liddell Hart, Capt. B. H., *The Tanks: The History of the Royal Tank Regiment*, Volume Two, Cassell: London 1959

Lucas, James, *Panzer Army Africa*, Macdonald & Janes: London, 1977

Pitt, Barrie, *The Crucible of War: Auchinleck's Command*, Cassell & Co: London, 2001

Playfair, Maj. Gen. S. O., *The Mediterranean and Middle East*, Volume III, HMSO: London, 1960

Quarrie, Bruce, *Afrika Korps*, Patrick Stephens: Cambridge, 1975

Stewart, Adrian, *The Early Battles of Eighth Army*, Leo Cooper: Barnsley, 2002

Verney, Maj. Gen. G. L., *The Desert Rats: The History of the 7th Armoured Division*, Hutchinson: London, 1954

INDEX